A MANIPURI GRAMMAR, VOCABULARY, AND PHRASE BOOK

A MANIPURI GRAMMAR, VOCABULARY, AND PHRASE BOOK

TO WHICH ARE ADDED SOME

MANIPURI PROVERBS
AND
SPECIMENS OF MANIPURI CORRESPONDENCE

BY

A. J. PRIMROSE, C.A.

OFFICIATING POLITICAL AGENT, MANIPUR

GYAN

Published by

Gyan Publishing House
5, Ansari Road
Daryaganj, New Delhi-110002
Phone: 011-47034999, 9811692060
E-mail: books@gyanbooks.com

Distribution Network
gyanbooks.com
India, USA, Canada, UK, Australia, France

ISBN : 978-81-212-3751-2 (PB)
First Published, 1888

2nd Impression 2020

Printed at: Gyan Press, Delhi.

The book at your disposal is the edition of an old book originally published long back. The Text quality of this book may not be at par as compared to our other books but many readers approached us to reprint this important book so that it could satiate their hunger. We request all the readers of this book to help us to improve its quality by providing the necessary text of those pages which are not properly visible. Your valuable support in this case will be highly appreciated and acknowledged and our future readers will be benefitted immensely.

A MANIPURI GRAMMAR, VOCABULARY, AND PHRASE BOOK

TO WHICH ARE ADDED SOME

MANIPURI PROVERBS

AND

SPECIMENS OF MANIPURI CORRESPONDENCE.

BY

A. J. PRIMROSE, C.S.,

OFFICIATING POLITICAL AGENT, MANIPUR.

SHILLONG:
PRINTED AT THE ASSAM SECRETARIAT PRESS.

1888.

PREFACE.

THIS little book will, I hope, supply a want which has been much felt ever since our annexation of Upper Burma. The only land route to Upper Burma from Assam and Bengal is through Manipur. The journey through Manipur occupies about a fortnight. Hardly any Manipuri knows any language but his own, so officers travelling through find great difficulty in getting at the different stages the supplies which they are in want of, owing to their inability to make themselves understood by the Manipuri officials. Manipur is now the head-quarters of an Assam regiment, and in all probability it will remain for some time to come a Military Station, owing to the healthiness of its climate, as well as to its admirable strategical position in the event of any outbreak on the frontier. The above reasons have made a knowledge of Manipuri of greater importance than in former years. With the object of assisting in the study of Manipuri, I have prepared a Grammar, Vocabulary, and Phrase Book of the language.

A note on the Manipuri Grammar was published by the late Mr. Damant in the Asiatic Society Journal, Part I., Vol. XLIV., 1875. This note gives in few words a clear statement of all the more important features of the Grammar. I have not hesitated to make free use of this note in the preparation of my Grammar.

In the vocabulary section, I have arranged the nouns under different headings, such as relationship, trades, &c., which is I think a simpler plan than jumbling up in alphabetical order a number of words having no connection with each other. The English phrases I have copied from Mrs. Cutter's Assamese Phrase Book. I have added at the end of the book a few Manipuri proverbs, and also a few specimens of letters in Manipuri in order to give an idea of the style of address adopted in such compositions.

In the preparation of this book I have been assisted by my head-clerk, Russic Laul Coondoo, and by my Burmese Interpreter, Purander Sing, who both deserve my best thanks.

A. J. PRIMROSE,
Political Agent.

MANIPUR :
August 1887.

MANIPURI GRAMMAR.

NOTE ON VOCABULARY AND PHRASE BOOK.

In the transliteration of the Manipuri words and sentences from the Bengali into the Roman character, the vowel sounds are represented as follows:—Short *a* is pronounced as *a* in comp*a*ny, long *â* as *a* in f*a*ther ; *e* unmarked as *e* in th*e*n, *ê* has the sound of *ai* in *ai*m, or *ey* in th*ey* ; *i* unmarked is pronounced as *i* in *i*n, *î* as in mach*i*ne ; *o* unmarked as in p*o*t, *ô* as in b*o*ne ; *u* unmarked as in b*u*ll, *û* as *oo* in m*oo*n.

MANIPURI GRAMMAR.

INTRODUCTION.

Mr. Damant in his Note on the Manipuri Grammar, published in the Asiatic Society Journal of Bengal, Volume XLIV., Part I., 1875, gives the following interesting review of the language:—"The Grammar of the Manipuri language is practically unknown at present, and the Europeans who have any acquaintance at all with it might be counted on one's fingers. So far as I know, there is only one book on the language, an English-Manipuri Dictionary, printed at the Baptist Mission Press in 1837, and this is now very scarce. The language is to a certain extent a written one, and formerly had a character peculiar to itself. Manuscripts in this character still exist, and it is even now used in Manipur for genealogies and family records, but all ordinary business matters are carried on either in Bengali or in Manipuri written in the Bengali character. I may note that all grammatical forms given hereafter are derived from the language as spoken at present, and not from the manuscripts, which, I am told, contain many obsolete forms, and indeed are hardly intelligible to an ordinary Manipuri. The Grammar is very well worth studying, and as it contains many peculiarities which are found as well in the allied dialects of the Kukies and the Koupooees, a tribe of Nágas who inhabit parts of Manipur and Cachar, it seems probable that the language of the Lushais and several of the Nága tribes may be derived from the same stock. But we hardly know enough of these dialects to pronounce an opinion yet; however, even if we grant that they are originally branches of the same stem, they have varied so much that they are now distinct languages and not mere dialects, and a knowledge of one is of very little use in learning another. A Kuki speaking his own language cannot be understood by a Nága, or a Manipuri by either.

"One of the first peculiarities which strikes one is the double possessive which is prefixed to certain nouns; thus—

Aigi ipa	...	My father.
Nangi napa	...	Your father.
Mâgi mapa	...	His father.
Aigi ikok	...	My head.
Nangi nakok	...	Your head.
Mâgi makok	...	His head.

"In these words the possessives, *i*, *na* and *ma* are prefixed in addition to the usual forms *aigi*, *nangi*, and *magi*; *pâ* is of course the Manipuri for father in the abstract, but practically it is never used except in the forms *ipâ*, *napâ*, and *mapâ*. This peculiarity is, as a rule, confined to words signifying relationship, as mother, brother, sister, and the like, and to those which signify a part of the body, as hand, foot, &c., and it is also used with a few words in very common use, as *yûm*, a house, *pot*, a thing. It is not generally used with words of two syllables, but there are exceptions, as *aigi iráipâk*, my country, instead of *áigi laipak*. These are general rules only, for nothing but constant practice can teach precisely in what words it should or should not be used."

The only difficulty in the grammar is in the conjugation of the verbs and in defining the exact meaning of the many forms for the present, past, and future tenses. I have arranged the grammar in a different order from Mr. Damant, treating first of nouns, then of adjectives, then of pronouns, and lastly of verbs.

Nouns.

The declension of nouns is very simple. The terminations are—

Nom.	Na, *as* mi-na	...	a man (*mi* alone is often used).
Gen.	Gi, as mi-gi	...	of a man.
Dat.	Da, *as* mi-da (*also* mingonda*)	...	to a man.
Acc.	Bû, *as* mi-bû	...	a man.
Abl.	Dagi, *as* mi-dagi (*also* mingondagi*)		from a man.
Loc.	Da, *as* maphamda	...	in a place.

* NOTE.—The form in *ngonda* and *ngondagi* is only used in the declension of *mi*, a man, and in the case of personal pronouns.

The plural in the case of human beings is formed by adding *sing* to the word and declining in the same manner as in the singular, as:—

Mîsing	...	men.
Mîsinggi	...	of men, &c.

There is no plural form for animals and other things. *Kheibit* and *pumna-mak*, all, or *yâmna*, many, are used to indicate plurality.

Gender, in the case of animals, is indicated by the addition of *laba* for the masculine and *amôm* for the feminine, as:—

Sâgol lábá	...	a stallion.
Sâgol amôm	...	a mare.

In the case of human beings gender is indicated by the addition of *nipa* and *nupi*, but only when the same word is used for both male and female, as:—

Macha-nipa	...	a son.
Macha-nupi	...	a daughter.

ADJECTIVES.

All adjectives end in *ba*, and an initial *a* may always be prefixed without altering the meaning, as:—

Good	...	aphaba, *or* phaba.
Large	...	achauba, *or* chauba.

Adjectives can be declined like verbs, as:—

It was very good="masi yamna pharé," where *phaba* has been changed into *pharé* to give the word a past meaning. *Ba* is changed into *bi* in the feminine. Adjectives have no plural form.

PRONOUNS.

The personal pronouns are *ai* or *ihâk*=I, *nang* or *nahâk*=thou, *ma* or *mahâk*=he.

The form ending in *hâk* is honorific. The plural is formed by adding *khoi* to the singular non-honorific form. Pronouns are declined in the same way, as *mi*, a man.

Singular.

Nom.	Aina	nangna	mâna.
Gen.	Aigi	nanggi	mâgi.
Dat.	Aigonda	nangonda	mângonda.
Acc.	Aibu	nangbu	mâbu.
Abl.	Aigonda	nangondagi	mângondagi.

Plural.

Nom.	Aikhoi	nangkhoi	mâkhoi.
Gen.	Aikhoigi	nangkhoigi	mâkhoigi.
		&c , &c.	

The demonstrative pronouns are—

Asi, *or* masi	this.
Adu, *or* madu	that.

Âsi is also used in the same sense as *adu*, as " which will you take, this or that?" = " kadai laubage asira âsira."

The interrogative pronouns are:-

Kanâ *or* kanâno	who?
Kadai	what?

Relative pronouns are not used. A verbal participle with ***asi* or *adu*** is used in the place of relative pronouns, as—

The man who came yesterday leaves to-day = "ngarâng lakpa mi adu ngasi chatkani."

VERBS.

The conjugation of the Manipuri verb is very complete. I know no language which has such a variety of tense forms to express present, past, or future action. Most of the varieties have distinct meanings of their own. Every verb has also a negative and interrogative form conjugated in all tenses except the interrogative future like the simple verb. The Manipuris divide the verb into present, past, and future tenses. They also have an imperative tense form Under the present tense forms they classify what in English grammar is called the perfect tense. There are no less than eight different present tense forms with corresponding forms for the past and future tenses.

There is no difference in the terminations of a tense, singular or plural, for the first, second, and third persons except in the imperative, which is irregular.

The subjunctive mood is expressed by a participle ending in *labadi* or *rubadi*; *labadi* is used when the verb root ends in a consonant, *rabadi* when the root ends in vowel.

NOTE.—The above rule for the interchange of *l* and *r* is also observed in other tenses, *r* is always used after a vowel, *l* after a consonant.

The present participle ends in *duna* as:—

Tauduna	doing.

The past participle ends in *khîduna* or *luduna*, as:—

Chatkhîduna	having gone.
Tauruduna	having done.

The future participle ends in *laga* or *raga* as "chatlaga," "tauraga."

The participle ending in *lingaida* or *ringaida* means at the time of doing a thing,—as "when I was going there I saw him" ="aina asida chatlingaida mâboo aina uram-mi."

The participle in *kadabagi* or *nanaba* is used to express a purpose, as, "you make preparations to go"="nang chatnanaba thaurâng tau."

Conjugation of the verbs TAUBA (*to do*) *and* CHATPA (*to go*).

Present Tense forms.		*Past Tense forms.*		*Future Tense forms.*	
Form I.—*I* or *li.*		*ê* or *lê.*		*gani* or *gê.*	
I do	tau-i.	I did	tau-ê.	I shall do	tau-gani, tau-gê.
I go	chat-li.	I went	chat-lê.	I shall go	chat-kani, chat-kê.
Form II.—*ri* or *li.*		*rê* or *lê.*		*ragani* or *ragê.* *lagani* or *lagê.*	
I am doing	tau-ri.	I was doing	tau-rê.	I shall be doing	tau-ragani *or* tau-ragê.
I am going	chat-li.	I was going	chat-lê.	I shall be going	chat-lagani *or* chat-lagê.
Form III.—*khî.*		*khî-ê.*		*khîgani* or *khîgê.*	
I do (at a distant place)	tau-khî.	I was doing at a distance	tau-khî-ê.	I shall do	tau-khîgani *or* tau-khîgê.
I go (referring to a distant place)	chat-khî.	I was going at a distance	chat-khî-ê.	I shall go	chat-khîgani or khîgê.
Form IV.—*khiri.*		*khrê.*		*khragani* or *khragê.*	
I do (excepting something in return)	tau-khi-ri.	I did	tau-khrê.	I shall do	tau-khragani *or* tau-khragê.
I go (expecting to return)	chat-khiri.	I went	chat-khrê.	I shall go	chat-khragani or khragê.

Form V.—*rui* or *lui*.		*rure* or *ruê*. *lure* or *luê*.		*ragani* or *ragê*. *lagani* or *lagê*.	
I have done (at a distant place)	tau-rui.	I have done (and finished at a distant place)	tau rure *or* ruê.	I shall have done	tau-rugani *or* rugê.
I have gono (ditto)	chat-lui.	I have gone (completed action)	chat-lure *or* luê.	I shall have gone	chat-lugani *or* lugê.

Form VI.—*rari* or *lari*.		*rare* or *rei-ê*. *lare* or *lei-ê*.		*rarâgani* or *raragê*. *larâgani* or *laragê*.	
I do (with a purpose)	tau-rari.	I did (with a purpose)	tau-rare *or* rei-ê.	I shall do (with a purpose)	tau-rarâgani *or* ragê.
I go (ditto)	chat-lari.	I went (with a purpose)	chat-lare *or* lei-ê.	I shall go (ditto)	chat-laragani *or* lagê.

Form VII.—*ram-mi* or *lam-mi*.		*ram-mê* or *ramlê*. *lam-mê* or *lamlê*.		*ram-gani* or *ram-gê*. *lam-gani* or *lam-gê*.	
I have done (not yet finished)	tau-rammi.	I have done (completed action)	tau-ram-mê *or* ramlê.	I shall have done (some doubt expressed)	tau-ram-gani *or* ram-gê.
I have gone (not completed journey)	chatlam-mi.	I have done (ditto)	chat-lam mê *or* lamlê.	I shall have gone (ditto)	chat-lam-gani *or* lam-gê.

Present Tense forms.		*Past Tense forms.*		*Future Tense forms.*	
Form VIII.—*ramli* or *lam-li.*		*ram-lê* or *lam-lê.*		*ramlagani* or *ram-lagê.* *lamlagani* or *lam-lagê.*	
I am still engaged in doing	tau-ramli.	I have done (completed action)	tau-ramlê.	I shall have done (for certain)	tau-ramlagani *or* ramlagê.
I am still engaged in going	chat-lam-li.	I have gone (ditto)	chat-lamlê.	I shall have gone (ditto)	chat-lamlagani *or* chatlam-lagê.

IMPERATIVE MOOD.

Do	tau.	Go	chat-lu.
Let him do	tausanu.	Let him go	chat sanu.
Let us do	taussi or taunasi.	Let us go	chatsi *or* chatnasi.

PARTICIPLES.

Present.		*Past.*		*Future.*	
In *dunâ* or *tunâ.*		In *khiduna* or { *rudunâ.* / *ludunâ.* }		In *ragâ* or *lagâ.*	
Doing	tauduna.	Having done	taukhiduna *or* ruduna.	About to do	tau-ragâ.
Going	chat-tuna,	Having gone	chatkhiduna *or* luduna.	About to go	chat-lagâ,

Participle in ringaida *or* lingaida=*at the time of doing a thing.*

At the time of doing	tau-ringaida.
At the time of going	chat-lingaida.

Participle in {gadabagi / kadabagi} *or* nanaba=*in order to do a thing.*

I am arranging to do it	ai {tau-gadabagi / tau-nanaba} thaurang tauri.
I am arranging to go	ai {chat-kadabagi / chat-nanaba} thaurang tauri.

Participle in rabadi *or* labadi=*if I do a thing.*

If you do it, I shall go	nangna tau-rabadi chat-kani.
If I go, I will tell him	ainachat labadi mangonda haigani.

Participle in banina *or* panina=*because.*

Because I did it he is pleased	aina taura-banina ma nungairê.
Because I went he was angry	aina chat-panina ma sâorê.

Participle in gadabâ=*must do a thing.*

You must do it	taugada bawei.

Verbal noun in bani *or* pani.

The man who does	tau-bani.
The man who goes	chat-pani.
The man who did	tau-khrabani.
The man who went	chat krabani.
The man who shall do	tau-gadabani.
The man who shall go	chat-kadabani.

These verbal nouns can be used in the different tense forms, but the three forms given above are in general use, the other forms are rarely used.

In sentences such as the following : "the work which is being done is good," "the work which has been done is good," the passive tense forms are expressed by participle forms preceding the noun to which they are related, as, "the work which is being done is good "="touribâthabak adu fai ;" "the work which has been done is good "=" taukhriba thabak adu fai." After words like *kari*=what, *karam*=why, and other interrogative adverbs, a form is used ending in *page* or *bage*, for example, "what are you doing ?"=" nang kari tauribage ?" "How did you go ?"=" nang karam chat-lubagé ?"

NEGATIVE AND INTERROGATIVE FORMS.

Each of the eight forms for the present and past tenses have corresponding negative and interrogative forms. There is only one future negative and interrogative form. It is unnecessary to give all the different negative and interrogative forms for the present and past tenses as only two or three forms are in general use. The conjugation of the verbs *taubâ* and *chatpâ* in their negative and interrogative forms is given below:—

NEGATIVE CONJUGATION.		INTERROGATIVE CONJUGATION.	
Present.		*Present.*	
Tauroi, taude	chat-loi.	Taubra, taurabrâ	chatlibra, chatpra.
Tauramde	chat-lammoi.	Taudabra,* taudrabra	chatloidra,* chattabra.
Past.		*Past.*	
Taudre, taurudre	chatte, chatlamdre.	Taurabra, taurambrâ	chatlurabra, chatlambra.
Tauramdre	chat ludre.	Taurudabra,* tauramdra	chatludra,* chatlamdra.
Future.		*Future.*	
Tauraroi	chat laroi.	Taugerâ	chat-kera.
		Taugedra*	chat-kadra.*
Participles.			
Tauradana	chat-tadanâ.		
Taurudraduna	chat-ludradanâ.		
Taudraga	chattragâ.		
Tauroidabagi	chatloidabagi.		
Taudrabadi	chattrabadi.		
Taudringaida	chattringaida.		

* NOTE.—These forms are all negative interrogatives.

MANIPURI VOCABULARY.

The Universe.

The Universe	তাইবঙ বানবা	Táibang bánbá.
God	লাঈ	Lâî.
Demon	হিংচাঃবি	Hingchâbi.
Spirit	হেল্লোই	Hellôî.
Fire	মৈঃ	Mai.
Water	ইসিং	Ising.
Earth	লৈঃপাক	Laipâk.
Air	নুংসিৎ	Nunsit.
The void	অতিয়াঃ	Atiyâ.
Cloud	লৈঃচিল	Laichil.
Fog	লৈঃচিলথাঃবা	Laichilthâbâ.
Sun	নুমিৎ	Numit.
Moon	থা	Thâ.
Stars	থবানবিচাক	Thabânbichâk.
Rain	নোং	Nông.
Lightning	নোংথাঙ কুপ্পা	Nôngthângkuppa.
Thunder	নোংখোংবা	Nôngkhongbâ.
Rainbow	চুমথাঙখানবা	Chumthângkhânba.
Mountain	চিঙ	Ching.
River	তুরেল	Turêl.
Lake	পাৎ	Pât.
Plain	তমবাক	Tambâk.
Island	ইথৎ	Ithat.
Jungle	নাঃরক	Nârak.
Forest	উমং	Umang.
Stone	নুঙ	Nung.
Wood	উ	U.
Day	নুংথিল	Nungthil.

The Universe.—(Continued.)

Night	অহিং	Ahing.
Darkness	অমম্বা	Amambâ.
Light	অঙ্গানবা	Angânbâ.
Dew	লিকলাঃতাবা	Liklâ-tâbâ.
Hail	লেল	Lêl.
Hoar frost	উন	Un.
Heat	অসাওবা	Asâobâ.
Cold	অইঙবা	A-ingbâ.

Mankind.

Mankind	মি	Mi.
Man	নিপাঃ	Nipâ.
Woman	নুপি	Nupi.
Boy	নিপাঃমচ্ছাঃ	Nipâ machbâ.
Girl	নুপি মচ্ছাঃ	Nupi machhâ.
Infant	অঙাংমচ্ছাঃ	Angâng machhâ.
Maiden	লৈশাবি	Leisâbi.
Old man	হন্নুবা	Hannubâ.
Old woman	হন্নুবি	Hannubi.
Widower	পাখ্রাঃ	Pâkhrâ.
Widow	লুখ্রাঃ	Lukhrâ.

Relations.

Relations	সাঃগৈ	Sâgei.
Father	ইপাঃ	Ipâ.
Mother	ইমাঃ	Imâ.
Elder brother	য়াম্মাঃ	Yâmmâ.
Younger brother	ইনাও	Inâo.
Elder sister	ইচেম	Ichem.
Younger sister	ইচন	Ichan.
Uncle	ইপন	Ipan.
Aunt (wife of above)	ইহ্মান	Imhân.
Uncle (father's younger brother)	ইতোন	Itôn.
Aunt (wife of above)	ইন্দোন	Indôn.
Aunt (father's sister)	ইনেম	Inem.
Son	ইচ্ছাঃ নিপাঃ	Ichâ nipâ.
Daughter	ইচ্ছাঃ নুপি	Ichâ nupi.
Husband	মবা	Mawâ.
Wife	মত্ত	Mattu.

Relations.—(Continued.)

Grandfather	ইপূ	Ipû.
Grandmother	ইবেন	Iben.
Grandson	ইসুনিপা	Isunipâ.
Grand-daughter	ইসুনুপি	Isunupi.
Father-in-law	ইকু	Iku.
Mother-in-law	ইনেম	Inem.
Son-in-law	ইমাক	Imâk.
Daughter-in-law	ইমৌ	Imau.
Brother-in-law	ইনাও নিপাঃ	Inâo-nipâ.
Wife's elder brother	ইবাঈ	Ibâi.
Wife's younger brother	ইশেন	Ishen.
Nephew	ইচ্চাঃ নিপাঃ	Ichâ-nipâ.
Niece	ইচ্চাঃ নুপি	Ichâ-nupi.

Parts of the Body.

Parts of the body	হকচাংকায়াৎ	Ha kchângkâyât.
Body	হকচাং	Hakcháng.
Joint	তাংসম	Tângsam.
Bone	সরু	Saru.
Veins	সিংলি	Singli.
Flesh	হকসাঃ	Hakshâ.
Skin	উল	Ul.
Fat	মহাও	Mahâo.
Hair	সম	Sam.
Pore	তুখোঙ	Tukhông.
Brain	থোপ	Thôp.
Skull	লবাঈ লেম্ফু	Lawaî *or* Lemphu.
Head	কোক	Kôk.
Forehead	লাঈপক	Lâîpak.
Countenance	মাইথোং মকোই	Mâithông makôi.
Face	মাই	Mâi.
Ear	নাকোঙ	Nâkông.
Eye	মিৎ	Mit.
Eyebrow	পিসুম	Pisum.
Eyelid	পা	Pâ.
Tear	পি	Pi.
Nose	নাতোন	Nâtôn.

Parts of the Body.—(Continued.)

Nostril	নাতোন মখুল	Nâtôn makhul.
Cheek	খজাঈ	Khajâî.
Lip	চিনবান	Chinbân.
Teeth	য়া	Yâ.
Jaw	চাইরুং	Châirung.
Tongue	লৈ	Lei.
Chin	খডাঙ	Khadâng.
Beard	কোঈ	Kô-î.
Neck	ঙকসম	Ngaksam.
Throat	খৌরি	Khouri.
Shoulder	লেংবান	Lengbân.
Arm	পামবোম্	Pâmbôm.
Elbow	খুনিঙ	Khuning.
Wrist	খুজেং	Khujeng.
Hand	খুৎ	Khut.
Nail	খুজিল	Khujil.
Finger	খুদোন	Khudôn.
Thumb	খুৎপি	Khutpi.
Forefinger	খুদোনবি	Khudônbi.
Middle finger	খুয়াই	Khuyai.
Third finger	খুৎনিংথৌ	Khutningthau.
Little finger	খুৎনাওবি	Khutnaubi.
Palm	খুবাক	Khubâk.
Fist	খুদুম	Khudum.
Back	নম্গল	Namgal.
Chest	থবাক	Thabâk.
Breast	খোম্	Khôm.
Side	নাক্কন	Nâkkan.
Stomach	পুক	Puk.
Navel	খোই	Khôi.
Thigh	ফৈগল	Phaigal.
Knee	খুউ	Khu-u.
Leg *or* foot	খোঙ	Không.
Shin bone	খুরাঈ	Khurâî.
Calf of leg	খুবোম্	Khubôm.
Ankle	খুমিৎ	Khumit.
Sole of foot	খুয়া	Khuyâ.
Heart	থমোই	Thamôi.

Parts of the Body.—(Concluded.)

Blood	ইঃ	I.
Sweat	হুমাং	Hûmâng.

Animals.

Animals	সাঃ	Shâ.
Lion	নোংসাঃ	Nôngshâ.
Tiger	কৈ	Kai.
Elephant	সাঃমু	Sâmu.
Rhinoceros	সাঃমুগন্দা	Sâmuganda.
Horse	সাগোন	Sâgon.
Buffalo	ইরোই	Irôi.
Bullock	সন	San.
Bull	কাও	Kâo
Cow	সনবি	Sanbi.
Dog	হুই	Huî
Cat	হৌঃদোঙ	Haudông.
Rat	উচি	Uchi.
Sheep	য়াও	Yâo.
Goat	হমেঙ	Hameng.
Monkey	য়োং	Yông.
Bear	সওম্	Sawom.
Pig	ওক	Ôk.
Deer	সজি	Saji.
Mitten	সণ্ডং	Sandang.
Wild buffalo	সন্দৌ	Sandau.

Birds.

Birds	উচেক	Uchek.
Fowl	য়েল	Yel.
Goose	কাংঙাঃ	Kângngâ.
Duck	ঙাঃনূ	Ngânû.
Pigeon	খুনূ	Khunû.
Snipe	চেকলাওবি	Cheklâobî.
Painted snipe	কাংদ্রুক	Kângdruk.
Partridge	উরেনবি	Urenbi.
Quail	সোঈবোন	Sôîbôn.
Paddy bird	উরোক	Urôk.
Water fowl	পাংকী উচেক	Pâtkî ûchek.
Dove	লমখুনূ	Lamkhunû.

Birds.—(Continued.)

Parrot	তেৱাঃ	Tenwâ.
Crow	কাক	Kwâk.
Peacock	ৱাঃহোং	Wâhông.
Sparrow	সেনদাং	Sendâng.
Beak	মচিন	Machin.
Wing	মসা	Masâ.
Feather	মতূ	Matû.

Fish.

Fish	ঙাঃ	Ngâ.
Fresh fish	ঙাঃ অতেকপা	Ngâ atekpâ.
Dried „	ঙাঃ অকংবা	Ngâ Akangbâ.
Crab	ৱ ইখু	Waikhu.
Shell fish	থরোই	Tharoi.
Concha shell fish	মোইবুঙ	Môibung.
Eel	ঙাঃপ্রূম (ঙরিণ)	Ngâprûm (ngarin.)
Turtle	থেংগূ	Thenggû.

Insects.

Insects	তিল্কাঙ	Tilkâng.
Earth-worm	তিলথোক	Tilthôk.
Caterpillar	তিল্খাক	Tilkhâk.
Butterfly	কুরাক	Kurâk.
Beetle	কোবি কাংজেৎ	Kôbi kângjet.
Ant	ককচেং	Kakcheng.
White ant	লৈঃসৌ	Leisau.
Mosquito	কাঙ	Kâng.
Spider	মী	Mî.
Fly	হয়িং	Haying.
Bee	খোঈ	Khôî.
Snake	লিল্	Lil.
Water-leech	তিনফাঃ	Tinphâ
Ground „	কাকফৈ	Kâkphai.
Flea	হুইরী	Huirî.
Bug	মাঃ	Mâ.
Louse	হিক	Hik.
Midge	তুমিৎ	Tumit.
Centipede	নাচল্	Nâchal.
Lizard	চুম্	Chum.

Trees, &c.

Trees, &c.	উপান্নাচিংবা	Upánnachingba.
Tree	উপাল	Úpâl.
Plantain	লফোই	Laphôi.
Mango	হৈঃনৌ	Heinau.
Jack	থৈঃবোঙ	Theibông.
Plum	হৈঃখাঃ	Heikhâ.
Fig	হৈঃবোং	Heibông.
Peach	চুমব্রৈঃ	Chumbrai.
Pineapple	কিহোম্	Kihôm.
Bamboo	বাঃ	Wâ.
Cane	লিঃ	Li.
Creeper	উরিঃ	Uri.
Flower	লৈ	Lei.
Bud	লৈ আপোম্বা	Lei apômbâ.
Fruit	মহৈঃ	Mahei.
Root	মরা	Marâ.
Branch	মসা	Masâ.
Leaf	মনাঃ	Manâ.
Grass	শজিক	Sajik.
Reeds	সিঙউৎ	Singût.
Kagorie reeds	সিঙনাং	Singnâng.

Metals, &c.

Metals, &c.	ধাতু	Dhâtu.
Precious stones	তম্ফা	Tamphâ.
Gold	সনাঃ	Sanâ.
Silver	রূপাঃ	Rûpâ.
Copper	কোঃরি	Kôri.
Iron	য়োৎ	Yôt.
Brass	পিথ্রাই	Pithrâî.
Bell-metal	সেল	Sel.
Lead	মিসী	Misî.
Tin	কোনঙৌ	Kôngou.
Sulphur	কণ্ডক	Kanduk.
Mercury	সনাঃহিডাক	Sanâhidâk.
Saltpetre	চোংখারমচং	Chôngkhâr machang.
Diamond	হিরা	Hirâ.
Pearl	মুক্তা	Muktâ.
Glass	মিংসেন	Mingsen.

Clothing, &c

Clothing, &c.	ফিরোন	Phiron.
Cloth	ফি	Phi.
Coat	ফুরিৎ	Phurit.
Dhotie	ফৈজোম্	Phaijôm.
Shawl	ইন্নফি	Inaphi.
Pugree	কোকয়েৎ	Kôkyet.
Cap	লুহপ	Luhup.
Petticoat	ফনেক	Phanêk.
Slippers	খোঙউপ	Khôngup.
Silk	কব্রং	Kabrang.
Velvet	খেমজি	Khemji.
Handkerchief	চিঁদৈফি	Chindaiphi.
Gamchá	খুদৈঃ	Khudei.
Cotton	লসিং	Lasing.
Thread	লং	Lang.
Tape	ফিগোপ	Phigop.
Needle	য়েৎতুম	Yettum.
Necklace	লিক	Lik.
Bracelet	খুজি	Khujî.
Pendant earring	চোমাই	Chômai.
Round earring	নাইন	Nâin.
Tiara	কৈজেংলৈ	Keijenglei.
Ring	খুদোপ	Khudop.
Nose ornament	নাসিকা	Nâsiká.
Arm „	তাল	Tâl.

Bázár Articles.

Bázár articles	কৈঃথেনগী পোৎ	Kaitengî pot.
Rice	চেঙ	Cheng.
Dhan	ফৌ	Phâu.
Vegetables	য়েলশান	Yelsâng.
Red onions	তিলৌ	Tilau.
White onions	চনম্	Chanam.
Peas	মঙ্গল হাবই	Mangal hâwaî.
Matikalai	সাগোন হাবই	Sâgon „
Fresh fish	ঙাঃ অতেকপা	Ngâ atekpâ.
Dried „	ঙাঃঅকংবা	„ âkangbâ.

Bázár Articles,--(Concluded).

Salt	থুম	Thum.
Red pepper	মরোক	Marôk.
Turmeric	য়াঈঙঙ	Yâingang.
Ginger	সিং	Sing.
Sugar	চিনি	Chini.
Oil	থাও	Thâo.
Milk	সংগোম	Sangom.
Dahi	সংগোম অফম্বা	„ aphamba.
Betel-nut	গ্বা	Gwâ.
Pan leaf	পান্না	Pânnâ.
Lime	সুনূ	Sunnû.
Tobacco leaf	হিডাক মনা	Hidâk manâ.
Smoking mixture	হিডাক	Hidâk.
Hookah	হিডাকফু	Hidâkphû.
„ tube	হিডাকফু মঙক	„ mangak.
Chilum	ঙান্থক	Ngânthak.
Hookah-stand	হিডাকফু মখোঙ	Hidâkphu makhông.
Cloth	ফি	Phi.
Quilt (razai)	কানথা	Kanthâ.
Pillow	মোন	Môn.
Matress	মোনবাক	Mônbâk.
Mosquito-net	কাঙখল	Kângkhal.
Bamboo mat	ফক	Phak.
Fire screen	মাইখল	Mâikhal.
Cotton	লসিং	Lasing.
Lota	খুজাই	Khujâi.
Brass plate	পুখম্	Pukham.
„ pot (katora)	তেংগোৎ	Tengôt.
Large brass cooking pot.	কোরফু	Korfû.
Bell-metal ditto	কোফরান	Korfân.
Brass necklace.	পিথ্রাঈ গীলিক	Pithrâi gîlik.
„ bracelet.	পিথ্রাঈ খুজি	„ khujî.
„ anklet.	পিথ্রাঈ খোঙজি	Pithrâi khonjî.
„ ring	পিথ্রাই খুদোপ	„ khudôp.
Wax	খোইরূ	Khoîrû.
Spirits	যু	Yû.
Eggs	য়েরুম	Yêrum.

Implements.

Implements	খুৎলাই	Khutlái.
Plough	লাঙ্গল	Lângol.
Yoke	পোৎপু	Potpû.
Iron share	লোঙখুম্	Longkhum.
Hoe	য়োৎ	Yôt.
Axe	সিঙজঙ	Singjang.
Spade (kurpee)	তোক	Tôk.
Long dao	থাঙজৌ	Thângjau.
Sickle	থাঙগোল	Thânggôl.
Chisel	পাইজা	Pâija.
Gauge	পাইজাঃ মাইকোল	Pâijâ mâikol.
Saw	হোঃরাই	Horâi.
Hammer	মুঙথং	Nungthang.
Nail	য়োৎপি	Yôtpi.
Adze	হাঙমৈ	Hângmei.
Gimlet	লেপলৈঃ	Leplei.
Scissors	কাটি	Kâti.
Mallet	থেঙগু	Thengû.
Harrow	উকাই	Ukâi.
Cart	কাংবোৎ	Kângbôt.
Loom	য়োঙখম	Yôngkham.
Comb	ফিসা সমজেৎ	Phisâ samjet.
Shuttle	পাংঙলদেম	Pângaldem.
Warp	ময়ুং	Mayung.
Woof	মফেন	Maphen.
Spinning wheel	তরেঙ	Tareng.
Oil-mill	সেক	Sek.
Net	ইল	Il.
Fishing basket	লোংউপ	Lôngup.
Sword	কবাকথাঙ	Kabâkthâng.
Spear	তা	Tâ.
Short dao	থাঙ	Thâng.
Knife	হৈজ্রাঙ	Heijrâng.
Gun	নোংমৈঃ	Nôngmei.
Pánji	সৌ	Sou.
Bow	লিরূং	Lirûng.
Arrow	তেন্	Ten.
Shield	চুঙ *or* চুঙকোই	Chung *or* chûngoi.

Implements.—(Continued.)

Tongs	চেগাপ	Chêgap.
Hand-shears	কাটি	Kâti.
Anvil	নুঙফান্	Nungphân.
Pincers	তুমসৎ	Tumsat.
Scales for weighing	পাঃবোৎ	Pâbôt.
Weights	খল	Khal.

House and Furniture.

House and furniture	য়ুমগী পোৎলোই	Yumgi potlôi.
House	য়ুম	Yum.
Room	কা	Kâ.
Verandah	খরবান	Kharbân.
Ceiling	ফিজঙ	Phijang.
Roof	য়ুমথক	Yumthak.
Post	য়ুম্বি	Yumbi.
Rafters	খাঙনবূ	Khângnabû.
Beam	খাংঙেন	Khângngen.
Stays	হুম্দাং	Hûmdâng.
Thatch	ই	I.
Bamboo	বাঃ	Wâ.
Wood	উ	Û.
Door	থোঙ	Thong.
Window	মিহুৎ	Mihut.
Approach to house	সুমাঙ	Sumâng.
Threshold	মাঙ্গল	Mângal.
Cane (bent)	লি	Li.
Bamboo ribbon	পয়াঃ	Payâ.
Garden	ইংখোলঃ	Ingkhol.
Brick	চেক	Chek.
Wall	লৈঃপল (লৈঃরং)	Leipal *or* leirang.
Lock	বাইখূ	Waikhû.
Key	সো	So.
Stable.	সাগোলসঙ	Sâgolsang.
Cook-house	চাকসঙ	Châksang.
Sand	লৈঙ্গৈ	Leingwei.
Chair	তাঙবল	Tângbal.
Table	মেজ	Mez.
Box	উপূ	Upû.

House and Furniture.—(Continued.)

Bedstead	কাংথোল	Kângthôl.
Glass lamp	মিংসেল থাওমৈঃ	Mingsel thâomai.
Glass	মিংসেল	Mingsel.
Basket	থুমুক	Thumuk.
Large basket.	সঙবাই	Sangbâi.
Machán for things	সগাই	Sagâi.
Sleeping machán	কাংথক	Kângthak.
Dhán-sifter	য়াংগোক	Yângôk.
Dekki	সুম্বল	Sumbal.
Dhán-pounder	সুক	Suk.
Earthen boiling pot	চফূ	Chaphû.
Ditto, small size	ইবান	Iwân.
Oven (choolha)	লৈঃরঙ্গ	Leirang.
Iron stove	য়োৎসুবি	Yotsubi.
Firewood	সিঙ	Sing.
Spoon	খাঃবৈঃ	Khâbei.
Iron pincers for lifting cooking pot.	চেগপ	Chegap.
Bag	খাও	Khau.
Broom	সুম্‌জিত	'Sumjit.
Mat	ফক	Phak.
Bedding	ফমুং	Phamung.

Trades.

Trade	খুৎনাইবা	Khutnâibâ.
Carpenter	উশাবা	Usâbâ.
Blacksmith	থাঙ জবা	Thângjabâ.
Goldsmith	কোনসবা	Kônsabâ.
Brazier	অহৈঃবা	Aheibâ.
Weaver	ফিশাবা	Phisâbâ.
Washerman	ফিসূবা	Phisûbâ.,
Tailor	ফুৰিৎতুবা	Phurittubâ.
Fisherman	ঙাঃথিবা	Ngâ-tibâ.
Potter	ফুসবা	Phu-saba.
Workman	অয়েকপা	Ayekpâ.
Syce	সাগোন সেনবা	Sâgon-senbâ.
Gwala	সংগোম সুম্বা	Sangôm sumbâ.

School.

School	লাঈরিকসঙ	Lairiksang.
Teacher	ঊঝাঃ	Ujhâ.
Pupil	সেবক	Sêbak.
Paper	চেঃ	Chê.
Pen	কলম্	Kalam.
Ink	কালি	Kâli.
Inkstand	কালিফু, মুকফু	Kâliphu, mukphu.
Book	লাঈরিক	Lâirik.
Page	লাঃমাই মবুক মনম্	Lâmâi mabuk manam.
Leaf of a book	লাঃমাই	Lâmâi.
Line	পংক্তি	Pangti.

Names of the Months.

Names of the months.	থাগী মমিং	Thâgî maming.
January	বাকচিঙ	Wâkching.
February	লাঙ্গাফাইরেল	Langâpbâirel.
March	লমদা	Lamdâ.
April	সজিবু	Sajibu.
May	কালেন্	Kâlen.
June	ইঙাঃ	Ingâ.
July	ইঙেন	Ingen.
August	থবান	Thowân.
September	লাংবন	Lângban.
October	মেরাঃ	Merâ.
November	হ্যাঙ্গৈঃ	Hyângei.
December	পোইনু	Poinu.

Days of the Week.

Days of the week	নুমিৎ চয়োন তরেৎ	Numit chayon taret.
Sunday	নোংমাইজিঙ	Nongmâijing.
Monday	নিংথৌকাঃবা	Ningthaukâbâ.
Tuesday	লৈঃপাক পোকপা	Leipâk pokpâ.
Wednesday	যুমশা কৈশা	Yumsâ keisâ.
Thursday	সগোনসেল	Sâgonsel.
Friday	ইরাই	Irâi.
Saturday	থাঙজা	Thângiâ.

Time.

Time	মতম্	Matam.
Morning	অয়ুক	Ayuk.
Midday	নুমিৎ য়ুংবা	Numit yunbâ.
Evening	নুমদাং	Numdâng.
Hour	পুঙজাঃ	Pungjâ.
Minute	মিকুপ	Mikup.
A day and night	অহিং অমা নুংথিল অমা	Ahing amâ nungthil amâ.
A pahar	য়ুথক অমা	Yûthak amâ.
A week	চয়োন তরেৎ	Chayon taret.
A month	থা অমা	Thâ amâ.
A year	চহি অমা	Chahi amâ.

Points of the Compass.

Points of the compass	মাইগৈঃ মরিমক ।	Mâigei marimak.
North	অবাং	Awâng.
East	নোংবোক	Nongbok.
South	মখা	Makhâ.
West	নোংজুপ	Nongjup.

Weights and Measures.

Weights and measures	চেঙ ফৌ ওনবা	Cheng phâo onabâ.

Note.—There is a table for rice (*cheng*) and another for dhán (*pháu*).

Rice.

One basket about 10 chitaks.	চেঙ উতোং	Chengûtong.
15 ditto about 10 seers	চেঙ মখাই	Cheng makhâi.
30 ditto about 20 „	চেঙগোক	Cheng-gok.

Dhán.

One basket about 12 chitaks.	ফৌ উতোং	Phau utong.
4 baskets about 3 seers	ফৌ বামোন	Phau bâmôn.
8 „ „ 6 „	ফৌ সাগোন	Phau sâgon.
16 „ „ 12 „	ফৌ লাইতং	Phau lâitang.
32 „ „ 24 „	ফৌ লিখাই (সনজাং;	Phau likhâi, *or* sana-jâng.

Dhán.—(Continued.)

64 baskets about 1 maund 8 seers.	ফৌ নাম্মা, সঙবাই	Phau nâmâ, *or* sangbâî.
2 sangbâis	পোং অমা	Pot amâ.

Miscellaneous Nouns.

Miscellaneous Nouns	মসক মমিং	Masak maming.
Ship	হিডিগা	Hidingâ.
Boat	হি	Hí.
Oar	নৌঃ	Nau.
Fence	সনবল	Sanbal.
Cultivation	লৌঃ	Lau.
Village	খুল	Khul.
Road	লম্বি	Lambi.
Friend	মরূপ	Marûp.
Enemy	য়েকনবা	Yeknabâ.
War	লাল	Lâl.
Coolie	পোংনেক হাও	Potnek hâo.
Load	হাওপোং	Hâopot.
Ladder	কৈঃরাক	Keirâk.
Bridge	থোং	Thong.
Medicine	হিডাক	Hidâk.
Charcoal	মৈঃতান	Meitân.
Bridle	খুর্জিরি	Khûrjiri.
Bit	য়াচল	Yâchal.
Saddle	সাঃবন	Sâban.
Stirrup	খুনেং	Khunet.
Rope	থৌঃরিঃ আচৌবা	Thauri achaubâ.
String	থৌরিঃ অপিসা	Thauri apisâ.
Comb	কোকহাৎ সমজেৎ	Kok-hât samjet.
Ditch	লাংখোং (খোংবান)	Lângkhong, khongbân.
A drop	ইসিং মরিক	Ising marik.
Drum	পুঙ	Pung.
Flute	বাশি	Bâsi.
Gain	তোংজবা	Tongjabâ.
Loss	ময়েংতাবা	Mayengtâbâ.
Corpse	অসিবা	Asibâ.
Mud	লৈঃখোম্	Leikhôm.

Numerals.

Numerals	মসিঙ	Masing.
One	অমা	Amá.
Two	অনি	Ani.
Three	অহুম	Ahûm.
Four	মরি	Mari.
Five	মঙা	Mangâ.
Six	তরুক	Tarûk.
Seven	তরেৎ	Tarêt.
Eight	নিপান	Nipân.
Nine	মাপন	Mâpan.
Ten	তরা	Tarâ.
Eleven	তরা-মাথোই	Tarâ-mâthoi.
Twelve	তরা-নিথোই	Tarâ-nithoi.
Thirteen	তরা-হুমথোই	Tarâ-hûmthoi.
Fourteen	তরা-মরি	Tarâ-mari.
Fifteen	তরা-মঙা	Tarâ-mangâ.
Sixteen	তরা-তরুক	Tarâ-tarûk.
Seventeen	তরা-তরেৎ	Tarâ-taret.
Eighteen	তরা-নিপান	Tarâ-nipân.
Nineteen	তরা-মাপন	Tarâ-mâpan.
Twenty	কুল	Kul.
Twenty-one	কুল-মাথোই	Kulmâthoi.
Twenty-two	কুল-নিথোই	Kulnithoi.
Twenty-three	কুন-হুমথোই	Kulhûmthoi.
Thirty	কুনথ্রা	Kunthrâ.
Forty	নিফু	Niphu.
Fifty	য়াঙখৈঃ	Yângkhei.
Sixty	হুম্‌ফু	Hûmphu.
Seventy	হুম্‌ফু-তরা	Hûmphutarâ.
Eighty	মরিফু	Mariphu.
Ninety	মরিফু-তরা	Mariphutarâ.
A hundred	চাঃমা	Châmâ.
A thousand	লিসিঙ	Lisıng.
Ten thousand	লঁখাঃ	Lakhâ.
A lakh	লঁখাঃ অচৌবা	Lakhâ achaubâ.
A quarter	মসুং	Masung.
A half	তংখাই	Tangkhâi.
The whole	মপুম	Mapum.

Adjectives.

Adjectives	মখল মখাই অয়াম্বা	Makhal makhai ayâmbâ.
Red	অঙাঙবা	Angâ-ngbâ.
White	অঙৌবা	Angoubâ.
Black	অমুবা	Amubâ.
Green	অসংবা	Asangbâ.
Blue	হিগোক	Higôk.
Yellow	নাপূ	Nâpû.
Orange	মেমান্‌বা	Memânba.
Purple	মংগরা মচূ	Mangarâ machû.
Pink	লৈমচূ	Leimachû.
High	অৱাংবা	Awângbâ.
Low	অনেম্বা	Anembâ.
Long	অশাংবা	Asângbâ.
Short	অতেন্‌বা	Atenbâ.
Large	অচৌবা	Achaubâ.
Small	অপিসা	Apisâ.
Broad	অপাক্‌পা	Apâkpâ.
Narrow	অখুবা	Akhubâ.
Thick	অথাঃবা	Athâbâ.
Thin	পআঃবা	Apâbâ.
Beautiful	নিঙথীবা	Ningthîbâ.
Pretty	ফজবা	Phajabâ.
Ugly	অথিবা	Athibâ
Elegant	অ:রম্বা	Arembâ.
Clean	অরূঃবা	Arûbâ.
Dirty	অনৈবা	Aneibâ.
Sweet-scented	মনম্‌ নুংশীবা	Manam nungshîba.
Stinking	নম্‌থিবা	Namthibâ.
Straight	অচুম্বা	Achumbâ.
Crooked	অখোইবা	Akhoibâ.
Good	অফবা	Aphabâ.
Bad	ফৎতবা	Phatabâ.
Ripe	অমুন্‌বা	Amunbâ.
Raw	অসংবা	Asangbâ.
Soiled	অমোৎপা	Amôtpâ.
Clean	অসেংবা	Asengbâ.
Defiled	অমাংবা	Amângbâ.

Adjectives.—(Continued.)

Hot	অশাবা	Asâbâ.
Cold	অইঙবা	A-ingbâ.
Strong	অকন্বা	Akanbâ.
Weak	অসোলবা	Asôlbâ.
Old	অমনবা	Amanbâ.
New	অহল্বা	Ahalbâ.
Agreeable (to the taste).	অহাওবা	Ahâobâ.
Disagreeable ditto	হাওতবা	Hâotabâ.
Sweet	অথুম্বা	Athumbâ.
Sour *or* acid	অসিনবা	Asinbâ.
Bitter	অখাঃবা	Akhâbâ.
Brackish	অয়াকপা	Ayâkpâ.
Soft	অথোৎপা	Athôtpâ.
Crisp	অমেঙবা	Amengbâ.
Tender	অনৌবা	Anaubâ.
Tasteless	অচম্বা	Achambâ.
Rotten	অপৎপা	Apatpâ.
Heavy	অরুম্বা	Arumbâ.
Light	অয়াংবা	Ayângbâ.
Fresh	অতেকপা	Atekpâ.
Dry	অকংবা	Akangbâ.
Sticky	অনপ্পা	Anappâ.
Level	মত্তা মান্নবা	Matta mânnabâ.
Even	অতেম্বা	Atembâ.
Circular	অকৈবা	Akeibâ.
Round	অতুম্বা	Atûmbâ.
Angular	মসুং নাঈবা	Masung nâibâ.
Square	চিথেক নাঈবা	Chithêk „
Deep	অরুবা	Arûbâ.
Shallow	অথেনবা	Athenbâ.
Bent	অকোনবা	Akonbâ.
Sharp	অথৌবা	Athaubâ.
Blunt	থৌদবা	Thaudabâ.
Much	অয়াম্বা	Ayâmbâ.
Little	খজিকতা	Khajiktâ.
Clever	অসিংবা	Asingbâ.
Stupid	অপঙবা	Apangbâ.

Adjectives.—(Concluded.)

Smooth	অনানবা	Anânbâ.
Rough	অঙপ্পা	Angappâ.
Far	অথাপ্পা	Athâppâ.
Near	অনক্পা	Anakpâ.
Old in age	অহল	Ahal.
Young	নহাঃ	Nahâ.
Dear	অতাঙবা	Atângbâ.
Cheap	অহোংবা	Ahongbâ.
Fat	অনৈবা	Aneiba.
Lean	ময়াঙ কংবা	Mayâng kangbâ.
Early	অঙনবা	Anganbâ.
Late	অথেঙবা	Athengbâ.
Merry	অনোকপা	Anôkpâ.
Grave	অসুক্পা	Asukpâ.
Decayed.	অপুম্বা	Apumbâ.

SYSTEM OF CALCULATING THE *SEL*, OR COWRIE.

All fractions of a rupee are expressed in *sels*, the only national coin in use. Pice are not current in the bázár. The *sel* is a small round coin made of bell-metal; 400 *sels* go to a rupee. Every 8 *sels* are called by the name for 100. Thus 8 sels=*châmâ*, the name for 100; 16 *sels*=*chani*, or 200; 24 *sels*=*châhûm*, or 300; 4 *sels* are called 50, or *yânkhai*; 80 *sels* are called *lising amâ*, or 1,000. There are 5 *lisings* in a rupee. I have given the nomenclature in use from 1 to 24 *sels*. After 24 the fractions of each series of 8 *sels* are the same. I have also given the name for each multiple of 8 *sels* as well as the name for each multiple of a *lising* up to 5 *lisings* which is the equivalent of a rupee.

Sels.

১ সেল মখাই অমা।
২ সেল অমা।
৩ সেল অমা মখাই।
৪ সেল য়াঙখৈঃ।
৫ সেল য়াঙখৈ মখাই।
৬ সেল অহুম।
৭ সেল অহুম মখাই।
৮ সেল চাঃমা।
৯ সেল চাঃমা মখাই।
১০ সেল মঙা।
১১ সেল মঙা মখাই।
১২ সেল চাঃমা য়াঙখৈঃ।
১৩ সেল চাঃমা য়াঙখৈঃ মখাই।

Sels.

১৪ সেল চনি সেন্তাবা।
১৫ সেল চনি মখাই তাবা।
১৬ সেল চনি।
১৭ সেল চনি মখাই।
১৮ সেল চনি ঙৈগক।
১৯ সেল চনি ঙৈগক মখাই।
২০ সেল চনি য়াঙখৈঃ
২১ সেল চনি য়াঙখৈঃ মখাই।
২২ সেল চহুম সেন্তাবা।
২৩ সেল চহুম মখাই তাবা।

Sels.

২৪ সেল চহুম।
৩২ সেল চাঃমিৱ।
৪০ সেল চাঃমঙা।
৪৮ সেল চাঃতরুক।
৫৬ সেল চাঃতরেৎ।
৬৪ সেল চাঃনিপাল।
৭২ সেল চাঃমাপন।
৮০ সেল লিসিঙ।

Lising.

১ সেল লিসিঙ অমা।
২ সেল লিসিঙ অনি।
৩ সেল লিসিঙ অহুম।
৪ সেল লিসিঙ মরি।
৫ সেল লিসিঙ মঙা।

Note.—One *sel* is called half a *sel* (*makhai sel*) and 2 *sels* are called one *sel*=*selamâ* 14 *sels* are expressed as 200 less one *sel*=*sel chani sel tâbû*. The nomenclature from 25 to 32, &c., is the same as from 17 to 24.

Verbs.

Verbs	মচৎ হাইবা	Machat haibâ.
Have	লৈবা	Leiba.
Be	ওঈবা	Woiba.
Remain	লৈবা	Leiba.
Do	তৌবা	Tauba.
Live	হিংবা	Hingba.
Die	সিবা	Siba.
Eat	চাঃবা	Châbâ.
Drink	থক্পা	Thakpâ.
Sleep	তুম্বা	Tumbâ.
Awake	হৌঃবা	Hauba.
Laugh	নোকপা	Nokpa.
Weep	কপ্পা	Kappa.
Speak	ৱাঃঙাঙবা	Wângângba.
Hear	তাঃবা	Tâ-bâ.
Know	খঙবা	Khangba.
Sing	ইশৈসকপা	Isei-sakpâ.
Dance	জগোঈ শাবা	Jago-isâbâ.
Walk	খোঙনা চৎপা	Khongnâ chatpâ.
Run	চেন্বা	Chenba.
Fall	তূবা	Tûba.
Stand	লেপ্পা	Leppa.
Sit	ফম্বা	Phamba.
Want	ৱাতপা	Wâtpâ.
Take.	লৌঃবা	Lauba.
Seek	থীবা	Thîba.
Give	পিবা	Piba.
Carry	পূবা	Puba.
Bring	পূরক্পা	Pûrakpa.
Take away	পূখীবা	Pûkhîba.
Lift up	থাংগৎপা	Thângatpâ.
Put down	থম্বা	Thamba.
Cut	কক্পা	Kakpa.
Tear	সেগাইবা	Segaiba.
Bite	চিকপা	Chikpa.
Pull	চিংবা	Chingba.
Push	ইনবা	Inba.
Strike	য়ৈঃবা	Yeiba.

Verbs.—(Continued.)

Kill	হাৎপা	Hâtpa.
Bury	ফুম্বা	Phûmba.
Burn	চাক্পা	Châkpa.
Love	নুংসিবা	Nungshiba.
Hate	য়েক্নবা	Yeknaba.
Fear	কিবা	Kiba.
Be angry.	সাওবা	Sâoba.
Quarrel	খৎনবা	Khatnaba.
Steal	হুবা	Hûba.
Buy	লৈঃবা	Lei-ba.
Sell	য়োন্বা	Yonba.
Work	থবক সুবা	Thabak suba.
Play	শান্নবা	Sânnaba.
Come	লাক্পা	Lâkpa.
Arrive	থুংবা	Thungba.
Jump	চোংবা	Chongba.
Fly	পাঙ্গবা	Pâiba.
Snore	নাঃখোক্পা	Nâkhokpa.
Sneeze	হাকথি খনবা	Hâkthi khanba.
Gape	হক্কাম চলবা	Hakkâm chalbâ.
Cough	লোক্খূবা	Lok-khûba.
Hiccough	থগোকপা	Thagokpa.
Whisper.	নাপচিক্না হাইবা	Nâpachiknâ haiba.
Call	কৌবা	Kauba.
See	য়েংবা	Yengba.
Ask	হংবা	Hangba.
Bind	পূনবা	Pûnba.
Loosen	লৌঃথোকপা	Lauthokpa.
Smell	নম্বা	Namba.
Be weary	ৱাঃবা	Wâ-ba.
Mend	সেম্বা	Semba.
Break	থুগাইবা	Thugâiba.
Sprinkle	চাঙ্গবা (খিক্পা)	Châiba *or* khikpa.
Catch	ফাঃবা	Phâ-ba.
Send	সিঃবা (থাঃবা)	Si-ba *or* thâ-ba.
Ride	তোংবা	Tongba.
Wish	নিংবা	Ningba.
Open	হাংদোকপা	Hângdokpa.
Shut	থিংবা	Thingba.

Verbs.—(Continued.)

Find	ফংবা	Phangbâ.
Think	খন্বা	Khanbâ.
Throw	হূল্বা	Hûlbâ.
Fill	থল্হল্বা	Thalhalbâ.
Be empty	অসংবা	Asangbâ.
Touch	সোক্পা	Sôkpâ.
Assist	পাংবিবা	Pângbibâ.
Learn	তম্বা	Tambâ.
Rub	তক্পা	Takpâ.
Kiss	চুপ্পা	Chuppâ.
Swim	ইরোইবা	Irôibâ.
Hunt	সাতান্বা	Sâtânbâ.
Remember	নিঙসিংবা	Ningsingbâ.
Begin	হৌবা	Haubâ.
Wash	ইরূবা (ফিসুবা)	Irûbâ *or* phisubâ.
Teach	তম্বিবা	Tambibâ.
Be stingy	লিক্পা	Likpâ.
Forget	কাওবা	Kâôbâ.
Cook	থোংবা	Thôngbâ.
Annoy	ওৎপা	Otpâ.
Build	সঙশাবা	Sangshâbâ.
Sweep	বাঈসিৎপা	Waîsitpâ.
Mix	নৈখাইবা (তক্পা)	Neikhâibâ *or* takpâ.
Dig	তৌবা	Taubâ.
Pour	হৈবা	Heibâ.
Reply	খুম্বা	Khumbâ.
Feel cold	নিংথম্বা	Ningthambâ.
Kick	কাওবা	Kâôbâ.
Pursue	তানবা	Tânbâ.
Descend	কুম্বা	Kumbâ.
Cultivate	লৌখ্বৈবা	Laukhweibâ.
Dive	ইরুপ্পা	Iruppâ.
Destroy	মাঙহলবা	Mânghalbâ.
Press	নম্বা	Nambâ.
Seem	মালবা	Mâlbâ.
Finish	লোইবা	Lôibâ.
Germinate	হৌবা	Haubâ.

Note.—In the pages previously printed long vowels in the vernacular were specially indicated by : (bisarga) put after them, but this has now been omitted as superfluous.

Verbs.—(Continued.)

Grow	চাওখৎপা	Châôkhatnâ.
Be thirsty	খোঁরাংবা	Khaurângbâ.
Light up	মৈথালগৎপা	Meithâlgatpâ.
Leave	থাদোক্পা	Thâdôkpâ.
Despatch	থিনবা	Thinbâ.
Complain	ৱাকৎপা	Wâkatpâ.
Distribute	য়েলবা	Yelbâ.
Hang up	য়ালবা	Yâlbâ.
Consider	ৱাখন্তৌবা	Wâkhantaubâ.
Request	হাইজবা	Hâijabâ.
Exchange	সিন্নবা	Sinnabâ.
Imprison	কৈসুম্বা	Keisumbâ.
Owe	লন্তোনবা	Lantônbâ.
Be dirty	তুগাচবা	Tugachabâ.
Worship	ইরাৎপা	Irâtpâ.
Attack	পাংগন থেকপা	Pânggan thêkpâ.
Taunt	য়ৈহৎপা	Yeihatpâ.
Abuse	চৈহৎপা	Cheihatpâ.
Cover	খুম্বা	Khumbâ.
Respect	ইকাঈখুন্নবা	Ikâîkhumnabâ.
Be ashamed	ইকাঈবা	Ikâîbâ.
Praise	থাগৎপা	Thâgatpâ.
Melt	মহিচেনবা	Mahichenbâ.
Tremble	নিক্পা	Nikpâ.
Occur	থোকপা	Thôkpâ.
Drive	তানথোক্পা	Tânthôkpâ.
Blow	কাম্বা	Kâmbâ.
Boil milk	সংগোম ঙৌবা	Sangôm ngaubâ.
Boil water	ইসিংলূম্বা	Isinglûmbâ.
Divide	খাইবা	Khâibâ.
Row	হিহোন্বা	Hihônbâ.
Breathe	নিংশাহোন্বা	Ningshâhônbâ.
Sew	তূবা	Tûbâ.
Grind corn	য়ামতক্পা	Yâmtakpâ.
Hide	লোৎপা	Lôtpâ.
Be extinguished	মুৎপা	Mutpâ.
Thatch	ইকুপ্‌পা	Ikuppâ.
Lean	ঙাবা	Ngâbâ.

Verbs.—(Concluded.)

Follow	ইনবা	Inbâ.
Cross (a river)	লানবা	Lânbâ.
Mend	ফোৎপা	Phôtpâ.
Point out	তাক্পা	Tâkpâ.
Float	তাওবা	Tâôbâ.
Trample on	নেৎপা	Netpâ.
Sharpen	ফেংবা	Phengbâ.
Clean	সেংদোকপা	Sengdôkpâ.
Clothe	ফিসেৎপা	Phisetpâ.
Graze	সনসেনবা	Sansenbâ.
Measure	খুদুপওনবা	Khuduponbâ.
Marry	লুহোংবা	Luhôngbâ.
Bear (children)	অঙাং পোক্পা	Angâng pôkpâ.
Snatch by force	মুনবা	Munbâ.
Surround	কোইরবা	Kôirabâ.
Wander about	কোইবা	Kôibâ.
Be pricked by a thorn	তিংখংয়ুবা	Tingkhangyubâ.
Sow	মরু হূনবা	Maru hûnbâ.
Stop	ঙাক্পা	Ngâkpâ.
Beget	মরু হূনবা	Maruhûnbâ.
Be pregnant	পুক-কংবা	Pukkangbâ.
Be blind	মিৎতাংবা	Mittângbâ.
Be deaf	নাপংবা	Nâpangbâ.
Stammer	লৈরোম্বা	Leirômbâ.
Be lame	খোংতেকপা	Khôngtekpâ.
Wrestle	মুকনানাবা	Muknânâbâ.
Fight	লালসোকনবা	Lâlsôknabâ.
Conquer	ঙম্বা	Ngambâ.
Meet	ওকনবা	Oknabâ.
Jest	পাওসিন্নবা	Pâosinnabâ.
Be able	ঙম্বা	Ngambâ

Adverbs.

Adverbs	চৎনবা খঙনবা	Chatnabâ khangnabâ.
Again	অমুক	Amuk.
Alike	অমত্তনি	Amattâni.
Already	হৌজিক	Houjik.
Also.	অদুসুং	Adusung.

Adverbs.—(Continued.)

Always	মহৌশা (লৈখাক)	Mahousâ (leikhâk).
Apart	তোপনা (তোংঙান্না)	Tôpnâ (tôngngânnâ).
Backwards	তুংদা	Tungdâ.
Below	মখাদা	Makhâdâ.
Before	মমাঙদা (হান্না)	Mamângdâ (hânna).
Behind	মতুংদা	Matungdâ.
Daily	নুমিৎ খুদিঙ	Numit khuding.
Downwards	কুমথবদা	Kumthabadâ.
Early	ঙন্না	Ngannâ.
Elsewhere	মফম অমদা	Mapham amadâ.
Hence	অসোমদগী	Asômdagî.
Here	অসিদা	Asidâ.
Hitherto	হৌজিক ফাওবা	Houjik phâobâ.
How	করম্না	Karamnâ.
Immediately	হৌজিক মক	Houjik mak.
Like	মান্ননা	Mânnanâ.
Little	খজিক্তা	Khajiktâ.
Monthly	থাখুদিঙদা	Thâkudingdâ.
Much	য়ামনা	Yâmnâ.
Namely	অদুমক	Adumak.
Never	খক্নত্তবা	Khaknattabâ.
Nearly	খরনঙাইরে	Kharanangâirê.
No	নত্তে (মাই)	Natte (mâi).
Now	হৌজিক	Houjik.
Often	হন্না হন্না	Hannâ hannâ.
Once	অমরক	Amarak.
Out	মপান	Mapân.
Opposite	মাইয়োক ননা	Mâiyôk nanâ.
Only	মক্তা	Maktâ.
Perhaps	করিগুম্বা	Karigumbâ.
Probably	ৱৈবা মাল্লে	Wôibâ mâllê.
Quickly	থূনা	Thûnâ.
Since	অসিদরক্তগী	Asidaraktagî.
Soon	খরলৈরগা	Kharleiragâ.
Sometimes	করিকরিগুম্বদা	Karikarigumbadâ.

Adverbs.—(Concluded.)

Somewhere	করিগুম্বা মফমৃদা	Karigumbâ maphamdâ.
Then	মাতুদা	Mâdudâ.
There	মাদরক্তা	Mâdaraktâ.
Thus	মরম অসিদরক্তগী	Maram asidaraktagî.
Together	লোইননা	Lôinanâ.
Unless	নত্তরবদি	Nattarabadi.
Until	অতুপকিমখৈ	Adupkimakhai.
Upwards	মথক লোমদা	Mathak lômdâ.
Very	য়ামনা	Yâmnâ.
When?	কদৌংগৈ	Kadaungei.
Well	ফৈ	Phai.
Whence	অদুদগী	Adudagî.
Whence?	কদাইদগী	Kadâïdagî ?
Where?	কদাই	Kadâi ?
Where	অতুদা	Adudâ?
Why?	করি	Kari ?
Yes	হোই	Hôi.
Yearly	চহি খুদিঙ	Chahi khuding.

Prepositions.

Prepositions.	মাঙতুং হাইবা	Mângtung hâibâ.
According to	মতুংইন্না	Matunginnâ.
Above	মথক্তা	Mathaktâ.
After	মতুংদা	Matungdâ.
Among	মরক্তা	Maraktâ.
At	দা	Dâ (affix).
Before	মমাঙদা	Mamângdâ.
Behind	মতুংদা	Matungdâ.
Below	মখাদা	Makhâdâ.
Beside	মনাক্তা	Manâktâ.
Between	মরক্তা	Maraktâ.
For	দমক	Damak.
From	দগি	Dagi (affix).
In, into	মনুংদা	Manungdâ.
Of	গি	Gi (affix).
On	থক্তা	Thaktâ.
Out	মপান্দা	Mapândâ.

***Prepositions.*—(Concluded.)**

To	**য়োবা**	**Youbâ.**
Till	**ফাওবা**	**Phâobâ.**
With	**লোইননা**	**Lôinanâ.**
Without	**নত্তনা**	**Nattanâ.**

Conjunctions.

Conjunctions	তিন্নবা হাইবা	Tinnabâ háibâ.
Although	হাইববু	Hâibabu.
And	অমসুং	Amasung.
As so	অদুম অদুম্না	Adum adumnâ.
Because	করম্না	Karamnâ.
But	তৌইগুম্বসুং	Tauigumbasung.
Else	নত্তরবদি	Nattarabadi.
For	করম্না, মরম্না	Karamna, maramnâ.
However	অদুমক্পু	Adumakpu.
If	অদুম্না, বদি	Adumnâ, badi.
Likewise	সু, অদুম্না	Su, adumnâ (suffix).
Or	বৈরবসুং	Wairabasung.
Wherefore	অদুনা	Adunâ.
Yet	তৌইগুম্বসুং	Tauigumbasung.

MANIPURI PHRASE BOOK.

English.	*Manipuri in Vernacular.*	*Manipuri in English Character.*
Stay about an hour	পুঙ অমারম ঙাইখো	Pung amâram ngaikhô.
I shall reside here about a year	চহি অমারম অসিদা লৈগনি	Chahi amâram asidâ leigani.
There are about 100	চামারম লৈ	Châmâram lei.
They stood about him	মাবু কোইদুনা লৈ	Mâbû kôidunâ lei.
They ran about the town	মাখোইনা খুল মনুংদা চেল্লম্মি	Mâkhôinâ khul manungdâ chellammi.
We will talk about this affair	থবক অসি ঐখোই ঙাঙ নগনি	Thabak asi aikhôi ngâng nagani.
The birds fly above our heads	উচেক ইথক্তা সুল অতিয়াদা পাঈরী	Uchêk ithaktâ sul atiyâdâ pâirî.
You have been absent 10 days	নঙ তরানি মরম কারক্তে	Nang tarâni maram kâraktê.
He abuses me	মানা ঐবু চথাংবা তোই	Mânâ aibû chathângbâ toui.
According to this he said	অসিগী মতুং ঈন্না মানা হাইরম্মি	Asigî matung înnâ mânâ hâirammi.
He wished to go, accordingly I dismissed him.	মানা চৎকে হাইদুনা ঐনা চৎ হল্লি	Mânâ chatkê hâidunâ ainâ chat halli.
It was on his account that I went	মাগী মরমনা ঐনা চৎপনি	Mâgî maramnâ ainâ chatpani.
He related the account	মানা বাফম অসি হাইরম্মি	Mânâ wâpham asi hâirammi.
I have made up the accounts accurately	হিসাব অসি ঐনা চুমনা তৌরম্মি	Hisâb asi ainâ chumnâ taurammi.
My head aches very bad	ইকোক য়াম্না চিকই	Ikôk yâmnâ chiki.
He went across the brook on a log	উতুপকী মথক্তা তূরেল লাল্লি	Utupkî mathaktâ tûrel lâlli.
The log lay across the stream	তূরেল ফৈগাক ফৈনা উতুপ অমা লৈরে	Tûrel phaigâk phainâ utup amâ leirê.
The tree fell across the road	লম্বি ফৈগাক ফৈনা উ অমা তূখরে	Lambi phaigâk phainâ u amâ tûkhrê.
It will be to your advantage	নঙ কানগনি	Nang kânagani.

English.	*Manipuri in Vernacular.*	*Manipuri in English Character.*
He saw a mango tree afar off	মানা হৈনৌ পানবি অমা থাপনা উরম্মি	Mânâ hainau pâubi amâ thâpnâ uraumi.
Are you afraid	নঙ কীব্রা	Nang kîbrâ.
Do not be afraid	কীগন্নু	Kîganu.
I am afraid that there will be wind	নুংসিৎ শিৎ কদবা মাল্লে	Nungsit shit kadabâ mâllê.
He found it after search	মানা থীদুনা ফংই	Mânâ thîdunâ phangi.
After he had gone, I arrived	মানা চৎ খ্রগা ঐনা থুংই	Mânâ chat khragâ ainâ thungi.
You may tell me afterwards	নঙ কোন্না হাইয়ু	Nang kônnâ hâiyu.
Do not come again	অমুক হন্না লাক কনু	Amuk hannâ lâk kanu.
He speaks again	মানা অমুক হন্না হাইরী	Mânâ amuk hannâ hâirî.
You must not go again to the bázár	কৈ থেন্দা নঙ অমুক হন্না চৎ কনু	Kai thendâ nang amuk hannâ chat kanu.
Come again in the afternoon	নুমিৎ য়ুংবা মতুংদা নুংথিল অমুক হল্লক	Numit vungbâ matungdâ nungthil amuk hallak u.
He is against us	ঐখোইবু মানা মাইয়োক য়াই	Aikhôibû mânâ mâiyôk yâi.
He leaned against the tree	উপান্দা ঙাদুনা লৈ	Upândâ ngâdunâ lei.
He ran against the fence	সনবনগী মথক্তা চেন্খ্রে	Sanbangî mathaktâ chenkhrê.
He is of age	মাগী চহি থৌ খনবা য়ারে	Mâgî chahi thau khanbâ yârê.
Her age is 15	নুপী অসিগী চহি তরা মঙা সুরে	Nupî asigî chahi tarâ mangâ sûrê.
He is very aged	মা য়ামনা হন্নুরে	Mâ yâmnâ hannurê.
He died six months ago	মানা সিবা থা তরুক সুরে	Mânâ sibâ thâ taruk sûrê.
It took place long ago	থৌ অসি তৌবা নুমিৎ মতম কুইরে	Thau asi taubâ numit matam kuirê.

The boat is aground	হি লৈপাক্কী মথক্তা থাংগৎ তুনা লৈ	Hi laipâkki mathaktâ thânggat tunâ lei.
They are alike	মা খোই মান্নৈ এ	Mâ khôi mânnei é.
Have you brought it all?	পোৎ পুম নমক নঙ ঙমনা পুরক লব্রা	Pôt pum namak nang ngamnâ purak labrâ ?
All men must die	মি ঙম নমক সির গনী	Mi ngam namak sira ganî.
What have you been doing all day?	নঙ নুমিৎ চুপ্পা করি তৌবগে	Nang numit chuppâ kari taubagê.
The paddy is all gone	ফৌ পুম নমক চাদিং তৌখ্রে	Phau pum namak châding taukhrê.
Pull all together	ঙম নমক অমুক্ত বৈনা চিং উ	Ngam namak amukta wainâ chiang u.
He is almost dead	মা সিগ তৌরে	Mâ siga taurê.
I have almost a hundred cows	ঐগী সনবি চামরম লৈ	Aigí sanbi châmaram lei.
He lives alone	মা মতোম্মতা লৈ	Mâ matômmatâ lei.
I went alone	ঐ ইতোম্মতা চৎলি	Ai itômmatâ chatli.
You must teach the children to go alone.	অংঙা সিংবূ মতোম্মতা চৎনবা বারক উ	Angâng singbû matômmatâ chatnabâ wârak u.
He ran along the bank	মা মপাল ইন্না চেলখ্রে	Mâ mapâl innâ chelkhrê.
They are already come	মাখোই লাকতুনা থুং লরে	Mâkhôi lâktunâ thung larê.
I have also ten horses	ঐগী সুং সাগোল তরা মরম লৈ	Aigi sûng sâgôl tarâ maram lei.
My brother also has several	ইয়াম্মগী সুং খর লৈ	Iyâmmagî sung khara lei.
They bring wood alternately	মাখোইনা সিঙ নোংমা নোংমা থৈননা পুরক ই	Mâkhôinâ sing nôngmâ nôngmâ thainanâ purak i.
Although he started, he did not arrive	মানা চৎতুনাসুং তৌ ই গুম্বসং য়ৌদে	Mânâ chattunâsung tau i gumbasung vaudê.
I shall dismiss him altogether	মাবূ ঐনা অমুক্তা বৈনা ইথোক্কে	Mâbû ainâ amuktâ wainâ inthôkkê.
You are always too late	নঙ লৈখাক কাবা থিল্লি	Nang leikhâk kâbâ thilli.

English.	Manipuri in Vernacular.	Manipuri in English Character.
It remains always here	পোৎ অসি লৈখাক অসিদা লৈ	Pôt asi leikhâk asidâ lei.
There is a bird among the branches	উচেক অমা উসাদা তোংই	Uchek amâ usâdâ tôngi.
Among many houses, that is the greatest.	য়ুম খৈবিক তগী য়ুম অসিনা হেল্নাচাওই	Yum khaibik tagî yum asinâ helnâ-châôi.
This is an ancient writing	লাঈরিক অসি অমনবনি	Lâîrik asi amanbani.
A man and a horse	মি অমগা অমসুং সাগোল অমগা	Mi amagâ amasung sâgôl amagâ.
The sun, moon, and stars	নুমিৎ থা অমসুং থবান বিচাকসিং	Numit thâ amasung thawân bichâk-sing.
Go and see	চৎতুনা য়েংউ	Chattuna yengu.
Will you go and bathe?	নঙ চৎতুনা ইরু জরু গেরা	Nang chattuna irû jarû gêrâ ?
They carried off the child and its mother.	মাখোইনা মমা মচাবু ফাদুনা পূখ্রে	Mâkhôinâ mamâ machâbû fâdunâ pûkhrê.
I will begin it anew	পোৎ অসি ঐ অমরক হন্না তৌবাহৌগনী	Pôt asi ai amurak hannâ taubâhauganî.
The Chinese caravan visits Ava annually	খাগীসিংনা অবা লৈপাক্তা য়েংগে হাইদুনা চহিখুদিঙ লাকই	Khâgîsingnâ awâ leipâktâ yenggê hâidunâ chahikhuding lâki.
Another man did it	মি অমনা তৌবনি	Mi amanâ taubani.
If you know, why do you not answer?	নঙনা খঙলবদি করিগী হাইদবগে	Nangnâ khanglabadi karigi haidâbagê?
Is there any reason?	থৌরম লৈব্রা লৈতব্রা	Thauram leibrâ leitabrâ ?
Has any one entered?	মি কনাগুম্বা মনুংদা চঙলকপ্রা চঙলকতব্রা	Mi kanâgumbâ manungdâ changlak-prâ changlaktabrâ ?
I cannot find any body	ঐ কনাগুম্বা অমতা ফংদে	Ai kanâgumbâ amatâ fangdê,
Is any thing the matter?	বা-থোক ইব্রা	Wâ thôk ibrâ?

I did not say anything	ঐ বা অমত্তসুং হাইদে	Ai wâ amattasung hâidô.
You must keep the fowls and ducks apart.	নঙনা ঙানুগা য়েঙগা তোপনা তোপনা খাই দোকতুনা থম্মু।	Nangnâ ngânugâ yengâ tôpnâ tôpnâ khâi dôktunâ thammu.
Give the coolies four annas a piece	পোৎনেকমন অমম মমদা সিকী সিকী পিয়ু।	Pôtnekman amam mamdâ siki siki piyu.
He is apt to break the dishes	মানা লিকলিগী পুখম থুগাইবা মহৌশানি	Mânâ likligi pukham thugâibâ mahaoshâni.
Are you well	নঙগী অনা অয়েক লৈব্রা	Nanggi anâ ayek loibrâ.
I am well	অনা অয়েক লৈতে	Anâ ayek loitô.
Are you angry?	নঙ সাওব্রা	Nang sâobrâ?
Who are you?	নঙ কনানো	Nang kanânô?
Are you not ashamed?	নঙ ইকাই দব্রা	Nang ikâi dabrâ?
He eats as he goes	চানা চানা চৎলি	Chânâ chânâ chatli.
He goes as far as the house	য়ুম য়ৌনা চৎলি	Yum yaunâ chatli.
He does as much as he can	মানা ঙম্বা মখৈ তৌই	Mânâ ngambâ makhai taui.
He did as he was directed	মানা য়াথং মতুংইন্না তৌই	Mânâ yâthang matunginnâ taui.
He has gone as he said he would	মানা হাইবা মতুংইন্না মানা চৎলি	Mânâ haibâ matunginnâ mânâ chatli.
He talks as if he were a king	মানা নিংথৌ ৱৈবা মরম হাই	Mânâ ningthau waibâ maram hâi.
As I do not know your character, I cannot employ you.	নঙগী মচৎ খঙদবনা নঙবু ঐনা থবক পিবা ঙমলোই।	Nanggi machat khangdabanâ nangbu ainâ thabak pibâ ngamloi.
I will go and ask	ঐনা চৎতুনা হংগনী	Ainâ chattunâ hangganí.
He asks for four rupees	মানা রুপা মরিদং পুগেহাই	Mânâ rupâ maridang pugehâi.
He is asleep	মানা তুমলী	Mânâ tumli.
There is a beggar at the door	থোং মনাক্তা চাকনিবা অমা লৈ	Thóng manâktâ châknibâ amâ lei.

English.	*Manipuri in Vernacular.*	*Manipuri in English Character.*
He stands at the foot of the tree	মানা উপাল মখাদা লেপ্তুনা লৈ	Mânâ upâl makhâdâ leptuna lei.
I cannot do it at all	মাসি ঐ খক তৌবা ঙমলোই	Mâsi ai khak taubâ ngamlôi.
Ah, you have come at last	হি, নঙদি হৌজিকনা লাকইবোরে	Hi, nangdi haujiknâ lâkibôrê.
I want at least ten	তরা সুনা ঐ লৌনিঙই	Tarâ sunâ ai launingi.
They all rose at once	মাখোই অমুক্তা বৈনা হৌগৎমনৈ	Mâkhôi amuktâ wainâ haugatmanei.
I did not awake	ঐ হৌদরি	Ai naudari.
Take this away	মাসি পুখ্রো	Mâsi pûkhrô.
Throw it away	পোৎ অসি জুনজেকখ্রো	Pôt asi jhûnekkhrô.
He has turned back	মা হল্লকলে	Mâ hallaklê.
He is reading backwards	মানা লাইরিক হনগৎনা পাই	Mânâ lâirik hangatnâ pâi.
This is a bad boy	নহা মচা অসি ফত্তবনি	Nabâ machâ asi fattabani.
Why do you write with a bad pen?	নঙ ফত্তবা কলমনা কদৌদুনা ইরীবনো	Nang fattabâ kalamnâ kadaudunâ iribanô.
Look for bamboos to build a house	য়ুম অমদং শানবা বা থীয়ু	Yum amadang sânabâ wâ thîyu.
Will he bring the basket?	মানা থুম্মুক অদু পুরক্কব্রা	Mânâ thummuk adu pûrakkabrâ.
He wants to be a priest	মানা পুরোহিৎ বৈবা পামই	Mânâ purôhit waibâ pâmi.
I went because you sent me	নঙনা চৎহলবা মরমনা ঐনাচৎ পনি	Nangnâ chathalbâ maramnâ ainâchat pani.
That beggar does not work, because he is lazy.	চাকনিবা আসি থবকসুদে করিনা হাইববু তলদুনা।	Châknibâ âsi thabaksudê karinâ hâibabu taldunâ.
That man has become insane	মি আসি ঙাওরকলে	Mi âsi ngâôraklê.
Make this bed well	ফমুং অসি নিঙথীনা সেম্মু	Famung asi ningthina semmu.

Where have you been?	নঙ কৈদা লৈরূ বগে	Nang keidâ leirû bagê?
Do not stand before me	ঐগী ইমাংদা লেপকনু	Aigi imângdâ lepkanu.
He had gone before I arrived	ঐ থুংদরি ঙৈদা মা চৎখিরমলে	Ai thungdari ngaidâ mâ chatkhiramlê.
He went before eating	চাদরি ঙৈগী মমাঙদা মা থোকখ্রে	Châdari ngaigî manângdâ mâ thôkkhrê.
Come before the sun sets	নুমিৎ তাদরি ঙৈদা লাকউ	Numit tâdari ngaidâ lâku.
I paid him beforehand	মাবূ ঐনা হান্না মচিন ঙৈদা পিরে	Mâbû ainâ hânnâ machin ngaidâ pirê.
We come to beg your pardon	ঐবু ঙাকপিয়ু হাইদুনা লাকপনি	Aibû ngakpiyu hâidunâ lâkpani.
I shall begin to build my house to-morrow.	ঐগী য়ুম সাবা হয়েং হৌগনি	Aigî yum sâbâ hayêng haugani.
There is a buffalo behind the hill	চিঙ বাংমা আসোমদা ইরোই অমা লৈ	Ching wângmâ âsômdâ irôi amâ lei.
He follows behind him	মাগী মতুংইন্না চৎলি	Mâgî matunginnâ chatli.
I do not believe it	বা অসি ঐ থাজবা লৈতে	Wâ asi ai thâjabâ leitê.
That boat belongs to me	হি অসি ঐগীনি	Hi asi aigîni.
Bring the box which is beside the bed	কাংথোলগী মনাকতা লৈবা উপূ অদু পুরকউ	Kângthôlgî manâktâ leibâ upû adu puraku.
It fell beside the road	পোৎ অসি লম্বি ময়াদা তাই	Pôt asi lambi mayâdâ tâi.
Besides this tribe is there another?	জাৎ অসি নত্তনা জাৎ অমা লৈব্রা	Jât asi nattanâ jât amâ leibrâ?
This is the best road	লম্বি খৈবিক তগী লম্বি অসিনা ফৈ	Lambi kheibik tagî lambi asinâ fai.
This house is better than that	য়ুম আসিদগী য়ুম অসিনা ফৈ	Yum âsidagî yum asinâ fai.
Do it better than this	মাসিদগী হেন্না অমরক ফনা তৌ	Mâsidagî hennâ amarak fanâ tau.
Do not stand between me and the fire	ঐগা মৈগা অনিমক্কী মরকতা লেপকনু	Aigâ maigâ animakkî maraktâ lepkanu.

English.	*Manipuri in Vernacular.*	*Manipuri in English Character.*
The river runs between two mountains	তুরেল অসি চিঙ আনিগী মরকতা চেল্লি	Turel asi ching ânigî maraktâ chelli.
This house cost between four thousand and five thousand rupees.	য়ুম অসিগী মমন রূপা লিসিঙ মরি মঙা বৈরে	Yum asigî maman rûpâ lising mari mangâ wairê.
Birds fly in the open air	উচেক সিংনা সুল অতিয়াদা পাইরী	Uchek singnâ sul atiyâdâ pâirî.
You are to blame	নঙ লান্বা থোকলে	Nang lânbâ thôklê.
Blow the fire	মৈ কাম্মু	Mai kâmmu.
The wind blows now	হৌজিক নুংসিং সিংলি	Houjik nungsit sitli.
Has the water boiled?	ইসিং শাহল্ব্রা	Ising shâhalbrâ?
Have you boiled the milk?	নঙ সংগোম ঙৌরব্রা	Nang sanggôm ngourabrâ.
Let the boatman go and bring the boat	হি পূরকউ হাইদুনা হিরান বদা হাইয়ু	Hi pûraku hâidunâ hirân badâ hâiyu.
He breathes the breath of life	মানা থবাই পানবা ৱৈবগী নিংশা হোল্লি	Mânâ thawâi pânbâ waibagî ningshâ hôlli.
The black jacket is handsome	ফুরিৎ অমুবা অসি ফজৈ	Furit amubâ asi fajei.
Bring me that book	লাইরিক অদু পূরকউ	Lâirik adu pûraku.
Take care, you will break it	নঙ চেকসিন্না তৌ মাসি কাইগনি	Nang cheksinnâ tau mâsi kâigani.
How broad shall I make this mat?	ঐবু ফক অসি কয়া পাকনা শাও হাইবগে	Aibû fak asi kayâ pâknâ shâô haibagê.
Give the broom	সুমজিৎ পিয়ু	Sumjit piyu.
I called my brother, but he would not come.	ঐনা ইনাওবু কৌববু লাকতে	Ainâ inâôbû kaubabû lâktê.
Are these two men brothers?	মবিঙা অসি মচি মনাওরা	Mabingâ asi machi manâorâ?
They all took hold, but could not lift	মাখোই পুম নমকনা পাইববু থাংগৎপা ঙমদে	Mâkhôi pum namaknâ paibabû thânggatpâ ngamdê.

He indeed hears, but he does not understand.	মাঁ নিঙথীনা তাববু বা লোৱা ঙমদে	Mâ ningthinâ tâbabû wâ loubâ ngamdê.
Buy six large boards	উপাক অচোবা তরুক লৈয়	Upâk achoubâ taruk leiyu.
He sat by the well	গোহাগী মনাক্তা মানা ফমই	Gôhâgi manâktâ mânâ pahmi.
Shall we go by land, or in a boat?	ঐ খোইবু খোঙনা চৎকদ্রা হিনা চৎকদ্রা	Ai khôibû khôngnâ chatkadrâ hinâ chatkadrâ?
He killed him by means of a poisoned arrow.	মানা মাবু হুগী তেন্না হাৎলে	Mânâ mâbû hugi tennâ hâtlê.
He will come by and by	মানা খর তপনা লাককনি	Mânâ khara tapnâ lâkkanni.
Call the syce	সাগোল সেনবা কৌ	Sâgôl sênbâ kau.
What is this called in Assamese?	অসিবু তেখাওরোন্না করি কৌবগে	Asibû tekhâorônnâ kari kaubagê?
Can you read Burmese books?	নঙ অবা লাইরিক পাবা ঙমব্রা	Nang awâ lâirik pâbâ ngambrâ?
Can you ride?	নঙ সাগোল তোংবা হৈব্রা	Nang sâgôl tôngbâ heibrâ.
I can ride very fast	য়ামনা কন্না থৌবা ঙমই	Yâmnâ kannâ thaubâ ngami.
Can you swim	ইরোইবা হৈব্রা	Irôibâ heibrâ?
I can swim, Sir	মহাশয়, ইরোইবা হৈতে	Mahâsay, irôibâ heitê.
He cannot come to-day	মা ঙসি লাকপা ঙমলোই	Mâ ngasi lâkpâ ngamlôi.
He says that he can come to-morrow	মানা হাই মা হয়েং লাকপা ঙমগনি	Mânâ hâi mâ hayêng lâkpâ ngamgani.
Light a candle	খোইরু থাওমৈ অমা থান গৎলু	Khôiru thâômei amâ thân gatlu.
Take care, and do not fall	লাইরেক কনু তুগনি	Lâirek kanu tugani.
Carry this to the chief	অসি সর্দারগী মফমদা য়৷উহল্লু	Asi sardârgi maphamdâ yauballu.
What is the cause of all this?	অয়াম্বা অসি মরম করিগীনো	Ayâmbâ asi maram kariginô?
Cause him to come here	মাবু অসিদা লাকহল্লু	Mâbû asidâ lâkhallu.

English.	*Manipuri in Vernacular.*	*Manipuri in English Character.*
He caused it to be brought	মাসি মানা পূরক হল্লি	Mâsi mânâ pûrak halli.
Cease to do evil	ফত্তবা তৌবা তোকলো	Fattabâ taubâ tôklô.
Certainly, how else can it be?	মাদু নত্তরবদি কম্না ৱৈগদবগে	Mâdu nattarabadi kamnâ waigadabagê?
Wipe the chair	চৌকি কন্থোকউ	Chauki kanthôku.
Can you change a rupee?	রূপা অমদং কাইথোকপিবা ঙমগদ্রা	Rûpâ amadang kâithôkpibâ ngamgadrâ?
I wish to change this boat	হি অসি ঐনা সিলনিঙই	Hi asi ainâ silningi.
Take your choice	নঙনা পাম্বা খল্লু	Nangnâ pâmbâ khallu.
He lives in the city	মা কনুংদা লৈবনি	Mâ kanungdâ leibani.
If the glass is clean, fill it with water, and bring it to me.	গিলাস অসি অসেংবা ৱৈরবদি ইসিং খর হাপ্তুনা ঐ ঙোন্দা পিয়ু	Gilâs asi asengbâ wairabadi ising khara hâptunâ ai ngôndâ piyu.
Clean the path	লম্বি সেংদোকউ	Lambi sengdôku.
Clear away the jungle	নারক অসি সেংদোকউ	Nârak asi sengdôku.
The water is clean	ইসিং অসি অরুবনি	Ising asi arubani.
To-day it is very cloudy	ঙসিদি য়ামনা নোংথিমংই	Ngasidi yâmnâ nôngthimangi.
This lattice-work is too coarse	ফৈরোই খারিবা অসি কন্দানৈ	Pheirôi khâribâ asi kandânei.
This cloth is very coarse	ফি অসিদি লং পোৌই	Phi asidi lang poui.
It is cold to-day	ঙসী য়ামনা ইঙই	Ngasi yâmnâ ingi.
Bring some cold water	ইসিং আইঙবা খর পুরকউ	Ising âingbâ khara pûraku.
I have got a bad cold	ঐদি লোক য়ামনা কন্না থুংই	Aidi lôk yâmnâ kannâ thungi.
What is the colour of this cloth	ফি অসিগী মচুদি করি মচুনো	Fi asigî machudi kari machunô.
Comb your hair	সম হাৎলু	Sam hâtlu.

I did not come	ঐ লাক্তে	Ai làktê.
Come here	অসোমদা লাকউ	Asômdâ lâku.
Let us commence our work	থবক সুবা হৌসি	Thabak subâ hausi.
Bell-metal is composed of copper and tin.	কোরিগা কোনডৌগা য়ান্নরগা সেল ওল্লি	Kôrigâ kônngougâ yânnaragâ sel ôlli.
Everything is in confusion.	থবক পুমনমক ওন্না তৈনরে	Thabak pumnamak ônna teinarê.
There has been considerable rain	নোংয়ামনা চুরে	Nôngyâmnâ churê.
There is a continual noise in this place.	মফম অসিদা ইতৎ তৎতনা নিল খোংই	Mapham asidâ itat tattanâ nil khôngi.
He acts contrary to the king's command	মানা নিংথোগী য়াথংবু সেরান্ননা তৌরে	Mânâ ningthougî yâthangbû serânnanâ tourê.
Is there a cook-house?	আদা চাকসঙ অমা লৈব্রা	Âdâ châksang amâ leibrâ?
She has a very bad cough	নুপি অসি লোকয়ামনা কন্না থুংলে	Nupi asi lôkyâmnâ kannâ thunglê.
They could not tell me	মাখোইনা ঐ ঙোন্দা হাইবা ঙমদে	Mákhôinâ ai ngôndâ hâibâ ngamdê.
Count the spoons	খরোই মসিঙ থিয়ু	Kharôi masing thiyu.
Buy a couple of ducks	ঙানু পুমা লৈরু	Ngânu pûmâ leirû.
Take off the cover from that dish	পুখম চাককুপইবা আসি হাংদোকউ	Pukham châkkupibâ âsi hângdôku.
He is very cunning	মাসি য়ামনা মমিৎমনা সিংই	Mâsi yâmnâ mamitmanâ singi.
Take a cup out of the cup-board	তেংগোৎ থম্বা ফান্দগী তেংগোৎ অমা লৌরু	Tenggôt thambâ phândagî tenggôt amâ lourû.
Give the curry	য়েনসাং অদু পিয়ু	Yensâng adu piyu.
Is the current strong?	ইসিং ইচেল য়ামনা কন্না চেনব্রা	Ising ichel yâmnâ kannâ chenbrâ?
This is our custom	মাসি ঐখোইগী হৌনবা মচৎনি	Mâsi eikhôigî haunabâ machatni.
Shall I cut it in two?	অসিবু অনি থোকসিরা	Asibû ani thôksirâ?

English.	*Manipuri in Vernacular.*	*Manipuri in English Character.*
Dare you ride on horse back?	নঙ সাগোল তোংবা থৌনা ফব্রা।	Nang sâgôl tôngbâ thaunâ phabrâ?
We sent the scholars home before dark	লাইরিক তম্বা অঙাং সিংবু মমদরি ঙৈদাময়ুমদা থাই।	Lâirik tambâ angâng singbû mamdari ngaidâ mayumdâ thâi.
She sends her daughter to our school daily.	মানা মচানুপিবু নুমিৎখুদিং ঐ খোইগী লাইরিক সঙদা থারকই।	Mânâ machânupibû numitkhuding ai khôigî lâirik sangdâ thâraki.
The ship goes day and night	মৈগী হিনা অহিংনুংথিল নাইদনা চৎলি	Maigî hinâ ahingnungthil nâidanâ chatli.
Rice is very dear	চেঙয়ামনা তাঙই	Chengyâmnâ tângi.
I owe a debt of ten rupees	ঐ রূপা তরা তোল্লি	Ai rûpâ tarâ tôlli.
Is this water deep?	ইসিং অসি লূব্রা	Ising asi lûbrâ?
If you should fall in, you would die	নঙ অসিগী মনুংদা তারম লবদি সিরমগনি	Nang asigî manungdâ târam labadi siramganî.
What is the difference between the two?	অনি সিগী মরক্তা করি তোপ্পা লৈবগে	Ani sigî maraktâ kari tôppâ leibagê.
The pronunciation is different, but the meaning is the same.	খোনফমদি তোপই, অর্থদি অমতনি	Khônphamdi tôpi, arthadi amatani.
The Burmese language is very difficult	অবারোন্দি য়ামনা লুই	Awârôndi yâmnâ lui.
He dips his finger in water	মাখুৎকি খুদোন অমা ইসিংদা লুপ ই	Makhutki khudôn amâ isingdâ lup i.
They are dishonest	মাখোই মচৎ ফত্তবা মিনি	Mâkhôi machat phattabâ mini.
The place to which he went is very distant.	মফম অদুদা মানা চৎখিবা য়ামনা থাপ ই	Mapham adudâ mânâ chatkhibâ yâmnâ thâp i.
Did you do it?	নঙ মাদু তৌরমব্রা	Nang mâdu taurambrâ?
How does he do	মাদু কমতৌরি	Mâdu kamtauri.

Do it, do it not	মাদু তৌ, মাদু তৌগনু	Mâdu tao, mâdu taugonu.
Do not go, do not forget	চৎকনু কাওগনু	Chatkanu kâoganu.
Do you know this?	মাসি খঙব্রা	Mâsi khangbrâ.
Have you done eating rice?	চাক চাবা লোইরব্রা	Châk châbâ lôirabrâ.
I have done, Sir	ঐ লোইজরে ঐজ্ঞা	Ai lôijarê agya.
I have not done yet	ঐ হৌজিক ফাওবা লোইদরি	Ai houjik phâobâ lôidari.
Have you done writing?	লাঈরিক ইবা লোইরব্রা	Lâirik ibâ lôirabrâ?
It is done	মাসি লোইরে	Mâsi lôirê.
This cloth is double	ফি অসি অনি লোল্লে	Phi asi ani lôllê.
It is doubtful	মাসি চিংনৈ	Mâsi chingnei.
He came down from the mountain	মা চিঙ কুমলে	Mâ ching kumlê.
Let down the sail	পাল থাদরো	Pâl thâdarô.
They sail down the river	মাখোই ইসিং ইচেল মতুং ইন্না হি তোংদুনা চৎলে।	Mâkhôi ising ichel matung innâ hi tôngdunâ chatlê.
Buy a dozen eggs	য়েরুম তরা নিথোই লৈয়ু	Yêrum tarâ nithôi leiyu.
Have you drunk medicine?	হিদাক থকলম্ব্রা	Hidâk thaklambrâ.
He dresses according to the English custom.	মানা ইঙ্গরাজিগী ফিজেৎ মান্না সেৎলি	Mânâ ingrâjigî phijet mânnâ setli.
The boatmen receive Rs. 4 each per month.	হি হোন্‌বা মি অমনা থাদা তলব রূপা মরি চাই।	Hi hônbâ mi amanâ thâdâ talab rûpâ mari châi.
Come early to-morrow morning	হয়েং অয়ুক ঙন্না লাকউ	Hayeng ayuk ngannâ lâku.
China is east of Bengal	খাগী লৈপাকতি বাঙ্গালা দেশগী নোংবোক লমদা লৈ।	Khâgî leipâkti bângâlâ desgî nôngbôk lamdâ lei.
I will eat and come again	চাক চারগা ঐ অমুক হল্লক কনি	Châk châragâ ai amuk hallak kani.

English.	*Manipuri in Vernacular.*	*Manipuri in English Character.*
You may take either this or that	নঙনা অসি লৌগে হাইরবসুং অসি লৌগে হাইরবসুং অমা লৌ।	Nangnâ asi lougê hairabasung âsi lougê hairabasung amâ lou.
Either you or he have told a lie	নবিঙ্গা অনিমক্তগী অমদি মিনম্বা বা হাইবা থোকলে।	Nabingâ animaktagî amadi minambâ wâ hâibâ thôklê.
He is the elder son	মাসি মচ্চা অহন্নি	Mâsi machâ ahanni
Will you bring the elephant?	নঙ সামু পূরক কেরা	Nang sâmu pûrak kêrâ?
No one else can manage him	মা নত্তনা মাবুকনাসুং থোদাবা ঙমদ্রে	Mâ nattanâ mâbûkanâsung thoudâbâ ngamdrê.
You must do the work, or else call another man.	থবক অসি নঙতৌ, নঙনা ঙমদরবদি মি অমা কৌ।	Thabak asi nangtau, nangnâ ngamdarabadi mi amâ kau.
Do you wish to go elsewhere?	নঙ মফম অসি নত্তনা করম্বা মফমদা চৎনিঙবা	Nang mapham asi nattanâ karambâ maphamdâ chatningbâ.
He did it to the end of life	মানা সিদ্রিবা মখৈ তৌরে	Mânâ sidribâ makhai tourê.
God has neither beginning rednon	ইশ্বরদি অহৌবসুং লৈতে অরোবসুং লৈতে	Iswardi ahoubasung leitê arôbasung leitê.
There is enough	ওক লে	Ok lê.
There will not be enough	ওক ফাৎলোই	Ok fâtlôi.
I have not men enough	মি অসিনদি তৌগদবা ওকফাৎলোই	Mi asinadi taugadabâ okphâtlôi.
This is boiled enough	থোংবা ওক্লে	Thôngbâ oklê.
He has entirely failed	মা থবক পুম্নমক তৌবদা খক ফবা ঙমদ্রে	Mâ thabak pumnamak taubadâ khak phabâ ngamdrê.
He is my equal	মাসি ঐগা চপ মান্নৈ	Mâsi aigâ chap mânnei.
Divide the money equally	রূপা অসি চপ মান্ননা য়েন্নৌ	Rûpâ asi chap mânnanâ yennou.

It is equally for your interest and mine	থবক অসি নঙগী ঐগী কানগনি	Thabak asi nanggî aigî kâna-gani.
I am especially anxious for this	অসিগী দমক ঐ য়ামনা খৌরাংনা ঙাইরে	Asigî damak ai yâmnâ khaurângnâ ngâirê.
Is this number even or odd?	মপূ কাইব্রা কাইদব্রা	Mapû kâibrâ kâidabrâ?
These boards must be made even	উপাকসিং অসি মান্নন৷ তৌবা থোকই	Upâksing asi mânnanâ taubâ thôki.
We should even relinquish our right, rather than quarrel.	খৎনাগদবগী সরুকতি অচুম্বা ৱৈরবসুং হুনজেক পনা ফৈ।	Khatnâgadabagî sarukti achumbâ wai-rabasûng hûnjek pana fai.
He did not stay even a day	মা নোংমতসুং লেকৃতে	Ma nongmatasung lektê.
Every one must give account of him-self to God.	মি ৱৈবা খৈবিকনা তৌরিবা থবকপূ ঈশ্বরগী মমাঙদা হাইবা থোকই।	Mi waibâ khaibiknâ tauribâ thabakpu iswargî mamângdâ hâibâ thôki.
God is everywhere	মফম পুমনমক্তা ঈশ্বর লৈ	Mafam pumnamaktâ iswar lei.
That man is exceedingly angry	মি অদু য়ামনা সাওরি	Mi adu yâmnâ sâori.
What is the matter with your eyes?	নঙগী নমিত্তি করিতৌরে	Nanggî namitti karitaurê?
Is the house far or near?	ময়ুম লাপপ্রা নকপ্রা	Mayum lâpprâ nakprâ?
This road is farther than that	মাদুদগী সরক অদু থাপই	Mâdudagî sarak adu thâpi.
Do not speak so fast	বা অসুপ থুনা ঙাঙগনু	Wâ asup thûnâ gnâangganû.
I have bound it fast	অসিবূ ঐনা কন্না পুল্লে	Asibû ainâ kannâ pûllê.
Did your father find fault with you?	নপানা নঙবু চৈহৎপ্রা	Napânâ nangbû chaihatprâ?
It is not my fault	ঐ করিসুং লান্দে	Ai karisung lândê.
Feed the kitten	হৌদোঙ মচ্চাবূ চাকপিজৌ	Haudông machâbû châkpijau.
I have found a few mangoes	ঐনা হৈনৌ খর ফংলে	Ainâ hainau khara fanglê.
Fill the goblet with water	তেংগোৎ অসি ইসিং থন্না হাপউ	Tenggôt asi ising thannâ hâpu.
Are not these oranges very fine?	কমলা অসি য়ামনা ফবা নত্তরা	Kamlâ asi yâmnâ falâ nattarâ?

English.	*Manipuri in Vernacular.*	*Manipuri in English Character.*
I wish to buy ome fine cloth	ঐ ফি অফবা খর লৈ নিঙই	Ai fi afabâ khara lei ningi.
You are an dle fellow, finish your work.	নঙ মি অতনবা ৱৈরে থবক অসি লোইয়ু	Nang mi atanbâ wairê thabak asi lôi-yu.
Make a good fire	মৈ য়াম্না থাগাৎলু	Mai yâmnâ thâgatlu.
You will set the house on fire	নঙ য়ুম মৈ চাকহনগে তৌরি বোরে	Nang yum mai châkhange tauri bôrê.
The first day of the fifth month	মঙা সূবা থাগী অহানবগী নোংমা	Mangâ sûbâ thâgî ahânbagî nông-mâ.
Give the first one you find to me	নঙনা ফংলবদি অহানবগী অমা ঐ ঙোন্দা পিয়ু।	Nangnâ fanglabadi ahânbagî amâ ai ngôndâ piyu.
You are not fit for a school teacher	লাইরিক তম্বা সঙগী নঙনা উঝা ৱৈবা মতিক ৱৈদে।	Lâirik tambâ sanggî nangnâ ujhâ waibâ matik waidê.
Your jacket does not fit	নঙগী ফুরিৎ হকচাংগা চাদরে	Nanggî furit hakchânggâ chádarê.
It is too large for you	মাসিদি নঙগীদি চাওমল্লে	Mâsidi nanggîdi châômallê.
This is for your brother	নয়াম্মাগী অসি ৱৈরে	Nayâmmâgî asi wairê.
I bought it for my daughter	ইচ্চা নুপিগী দমক অসি ঐনা লৈরে	Ichâ nupigî damak asi ainâ leirê.
I will sell it for a rupee	মাসি রূপা অমত্তনা য়োনগে	Mâsi rûpâ amattanâ yôngê.
He forbids your going	নঙনা চৎপদি কাইথোকপিরে	Nangnâ chatpadi kâithôkpirê.
He looks like a foreigner	মি অসিদি লৈপাক অতৈগী ৱৈরব মাল্লে	Mi asidi laipâk ataigî wairaba mâllê.
I forgot it, Sir	মাসি ঐ কাওরে ঐজ্ঞা	Mâsi ai kâorê agyâ.
Go forward	মাঙদা চৎলু	Mângdâ chatlu.
He fell from the top of the mast	মা মস্তুনগী মতোন্দগী তারে	Mâ mastungî matôndagî târê.
He comes from the city	মা ইনফান্দগী লাকলী	Mâ infândagî lâklî,

I heard this story from the villagers	লবাই দগী মিসিংনা ৱারি অসি লিহুনা ঐনা তাহৌই	Lawâi dagî misingnâ wâri asi li-dunâ ainâ tâhaui.
He was absent from April till September.	মাদি সজিবুদগী হৌদুনা লাংবন ফাওবা লাক্‌তে।	Mâdi sajibudagî haudunâ lângban phâôbâ laktê.
He marches in front of his army	মানা তেংগোল মিয়াম চৎপগী মাংদা চৎলি।	Mânâ tenggôl miyâm chatpagî mângdâ chatli.
This house is full of smoke	ইমুং অসিগি মনুংদা মৈ খুনা থল্লে	Imung asigi manungdâ mai khûnâ thallê.
Is this cask empty or full?	পিপা অসি সংলীব্রা থল্লীব্রা	Pipâ asi sanglîbrâ thallîbrâ.
It is nearly full	থল গদবা খর ৱাৎলী	Thal gadabâ khara wâtlî.
This house is farther from the city than mine.	ঐগী য়ুমদগী য়ুম অসি ইনফান্দগী য়ামনা লাপই	Aigî yumdagî yum asi inphândagî yâmnâ lâpi.
You must look further	অদুদগী হেন্না থাপনা য়েংবা থোকই	Adudagi hênnâ thâpnâ yêngbâ thôki.
Do you know there is to be future judgment?	হয়েং অমুক্কী মপোক্তা মানা তৌবা মতুংইন্না লাইনা নোংদমবিরক-কদবা অদু নঙ খংব্রা।	Hayeng amukkî mapôktâ mânâ toubâ matunginnâ lâinâ nongdambirak-kadabâ adu nang khangbrâ?
Go quietly	তপনা চৎলু	Tapnâ chatlu.
What did you get? I got fifteen fowls	নঙ করি ফংবগে : য়েন তরামঙা ফংলে	Nang kari fangbagê : yên tarâmangâ fanglê.
Give them to me	পুম নমক অদু ঐ ঙোন্দা পিয়ু	Pum namak adu ai ngôndâ piyu.
I have given them to the khansama	ঙম নমক ঐনা খানসামাদা পিক্রে	Ngam namak ainâ khânsâmâdâ pi-krê.
Give a small spoon	খাবৈ অপিসা অমা পিয়ু	Khâbai apisâ amâ piyu.

English.	*Manipuri in Vernacular.*	*Manipuri in English Character.*
Go thou, go there	চৎলু, অসুম চৎলু	Chatlu, asum chatlu.
I go, thou goest, he goes	ঐচৎলি, নঙসুং চৎলি, মাসুং চৎলি	Aichatli, nangsung chatli, mâsung chatli.
We go, ye go, they go	ঐ খোই চৎলি, নঙখোইসুং চৎলি, মাখোইসুং চৎলি।	Ai khôi chatli, nangkhôisung chatli, mâkhôisung chatli.
Did you go? I did not go	নঙ চৎলূব্রা ? ঐ চৎলূদে	Nang chatlûbrâ? ai chatlûdê.
You will go, won't you?	নঙ চৎকদবা নত্তরা	Nang chatkadabâ nattarâ?
I will go, good bye, Sir	ঐ চৎকনি, সল্লাম ঐজ্ঞা	Ai chatkani, sallâm agya.
He has gone, they have gone	মা চৎখ্রে, মাখোইসুং চৎখ্রে	Mâ chatkhrê, mâkhôisung chatkhrê.
I had gone, he had gone	ঐ চৎলম্মি, মাসুং চৎলম্মি	Ai chatlammi, mâsung chatlammi.
My lamp has gone out	ঐগী থাওমৈ মুৎখ্রে	Aigî thâômai mutkhrê.
It is not good to drink spirit	য়ুথকপা ফত্তে	Yuthakpâ fattê.
This is a good girl	নুপি মচা অসি মচৎ ফৈ	Nupi machâ asi machat fai.
This man is a great man	মি অসি অচৌবা মিনি	Mi asi achaubâ mini.
He has a great many servants	মাগী মনাই য়ামনা লৈ	Mâgî manâi yâmnâ lei.
He is the greatest spendthrift I ever saw	অসিদগী হেন্না পিগনবা মি ঐ খক উদে	Asidagî hennâ piganbâ mi ai khak udê.
Grind this wheat in the mill	গেহু অসি কোন্দা য়াম তকউ	Gehû asi kôndâ yâm taku.
He is in the habit of lying	মিনম্বা বা হাইগনবা মিনি	Minambâ wâ hâiganbâ mini.
I had, thou hadst, he had	ঐ ঙোন্দা লৈরম্বা, নঙঙোন্দা লৈরম্বা, মাঙোন্দা লৈরম্বা।	Ai ngôndâ leirambâ, nangngôndâ leirambâ, mângôndâ leirambâ.
He had received it	মানা মাসি ফংহৌই	Mânâ mâsi fanghaui.

Divide that pine-apple, and give me half.	কিহোম অসি খাইদোকতুনা ঐ ঙোন্দা তংখাই পিয়ু।	Kihôm asi khaidôktunâ ai ngôndâ tangkhâi piyu.
One and half	অমা মখাই	Amâ makhâi.
Give me back half a rupee	রূপা মখাই হনবিয়ু	Rûpâ makhâi hanbiyu.
I want a handful of raisins	কিসমিস ঐ ঙোন্দা খুয়া অমা পিয়ু	Kismis ai ngondâ khuyâ amâ piyu.
He directs you to put a handle in that hoe.	নঙবু য়োৎ মখোক অসি পাল্লু হাইদুনা হুকুম পিয়ে।	Nangbû yôt makhôk asi pâllu hâidunâ hukum piyê.
This woman is handsome	নুপি অসি নিঙথিজৈ	Nupi asi ningthijei.
He is very handy at work	মানা থবক তৌবদা য়ামনা ফৈ	Mânâ thabak taubadâ yâmnâ fai.
Hang up that cloth	ফি আসি য়াল্লু	Phi âsi yâllu.
I happened to meet him	মাবূ খঙহৌদনা ঐনা ফংলে	Mâbû khanghandanâ ainâ fanglê.
This man is the happiest person in the world.	মা আসি তাঈবঙবান বদা খবাইদগী হেন্না নুঙাই।	Mâ âsi tâibangbân badâ khawâidagî hennâ nungâi.
I can hardly spare this book	লাঈরিক অসি পিগদবা ঐগী য়ামনা লুই	Lâirik asi pigadabâ aigî yâmnâ lui.
Hark ! do you hear it thunder	তাও ! নঙ নোংখোংবা তাব্রা	Tâo ! nang nôngkhôngbâ tâbrâ.
The bird has flown	উচেক পাঈখ্রে	Uchek pâikhrê.
Has the horse been fed with paddy ?	সাগোনবূ ফৌ পিজরব্রা	Sâgônbû fau pijarabrâ ?
Has the horse done drinking ?	সাগোন ইসিং পিথকপা লোইরব্রা	Sâgôn ising thakpâ lôirabrâ ?
I have, thou hast, he has	ঐগী লৈ, নঙ্গী লৈ, মাগী লৈ	Aigî lei, nangî lei, mâgî lei.
We have had, they have had	ঐখোইগী লৈরম্মি মাখোইগী লৈরম্মিই	Aikhoigî leirammi mâkhôigî leirammi.
Have you a fever ?	নঙ অরুম হৌব্রা	Nang arum haubrâ ?
What have you ?	নঙ্গী করি লৈবগে	Nangî kari leibagê.
Have you been to the village ?	নঙ লবাইদা চৎলুব্রা	Nang lawâidâ chatlubrâ ?

English.	*Manipuri in Vernacular.*	*Manipuri in English Character.*
Have you done drinking tea?	নঙ চা থকপা লোইরব্রা	Nang châ thakpâ loirabrâ ?
Having hid what he had stolen, he ran off.	হুখীবা পোৎ অদু লোৎলমদুনা মা চেনখ্রে	Hukhîbâ pôt adu lôtlamdunâ mâ chenkhrê.
Having said thus, he departed	অসুমনা বা হাইরমদুনা চৎখ্রে	Asumnâ wâ hairamdunâ chatkhrê.
Does your head ache?	নঙ্গী নকোক চিকপ্রা	Nangî nakôk chikprâ ?
I do not hear you	ঐ নঙ্গী বা তাদে	Ai nangî wâ tâdê.
Heat some water	ইসিং খর শাহল্লু	Ising khara sâhallu.
This box is very heavy, I cannot lift it.	উপু অসি য়াম্না লুমই ঐ থাংগৎপা ঙমদে	Upu asi yâmnâ lumi ai thânggatpâ ngamdê.
He was very heedless	মা করিসুং নিঙবা লৈতে	Mâ karisung ningbâ leitê.
Have the goodness to help me	ঐবু থৌজান বিদুনা খরা পাংবিয়ু	Aibû thaujân bidunâ kharâ pângbiyu.
Go hence	অসিদগী চৎখ্রো	Asidagî chatkhrô.
Look here	অসি য়েংউ	Asi yengu.
Hereafter I shall not do as I have done heretofore.	অদুমনা মমাঙদা ঐ তৌখ্রে মতুংদদি তৌররোই।	Adumnâ mamângdâ ai taukhrê matungdadi taurarôi.
This book was hers	লাইরিক অসি নুপি অসিগী লৈরমই	Lâirik asi nupi asigî leirami.
The robbers hid their plunder in the wood.	ডাকু তৌবা মিনা পোৎহদুনা উরক অসোঙবদা লোৎলি।	Dâkû taubâ minâ pôthudunâ urak asôngbadâ lôtli.
That tree is forty cubits high	উপাল অসি খুদুপ নিফু বাংই	Upâl asi khudup nifu wângi.
The highest mountain	চিঙ খৈবিকতগী চিঙ অসিনা বাংই	Ching khaibiktagî ching asinâ wângi.

She gave him her book	নুপি মহাক্কী লাঈরিক অদু মাঙোন্দা পিরে	Nupi mahâkkî lâîrik adu mângôndâ pirê.
It is now his	নিপা অদুগী মাসি হৌজিক বৈরে	Nipâ adugî mâsi houjik wairê.
He himself went	মা চৎখ্রে	Mâ chatkhrê.
He killed himself	মানা মথন্না হাৎলি	Mânâ mathannâ hâtli.
I wish to hire four carpenters	উসাবা মরিদং নেকনিঙই	Usâbâ maridang nekningi.
Hitherto I have not been able to find any.	হৌজিক ফাওবা মি অমতসুং থীবা খঙদে	Haujik fâôbâ mi amatasung thîbâ khangdê.
Shoot so as to hit the bottle	লিকলি আসি পান্নবা নোংমৈ কাপউ	Likli âsi pânnabâ nôngmai kâpu.
The canoe will not hold twenty maunds	হি অসি মন কুল চল্লোই	Hi asi man kul challôi.
This man is honest	মি অসি মচৎ ফবা মিনি	Mi asi machat fabâ mini.
The house is built at the entrance of the road.	য়ুম অসি লমজিন্দা শারমই	Yum asi lamjindâ sârami.
I hope your father will soon recover	ঐনা নিঙবদি নপানা নারিবা অদু নুমিৎ খর লৈরগা ফগনি।	Ainâ ningbadi napânâ nâribâ adu numit khara leiragâ fagani.
How are you?	নঙ করম তৌরিবগে	Nang karam tauribagê.
How can you do it?	নঙ করম তৌবা ঙমগদবগে	Nang karam taubâ ngamgadabagê.
How great?	কয়া চাওবনো	Kayâ châobanô.
How do you call it in Assamese?	তেখাও রোন্দা করম হাইবগে	Tekhâo rôndâ karam hâibagê.
If this is the case, how can I stop?	অসুম তৌরবদি ঐ অসিদা করম লৈ গদবগে	Asum taurabadi ai asidâ karam lei gadabagê.
I know how to paint	ঐ মচু সেম্বা হৈ	Ai machu sembâ hai.
How thick is this board?	উপাক অসি কয়া থাবগে	Upâk asi kayâ thâbagê.
How far is your house from here?	নঙগী নয়ুম অসিদগী কয়া থাপ্পগে	Nanggî nayum asidagî kayâ thâppagê.

English.	*Manipuri in Vernacular.*	*Manipuri in English Character.*
How much was the price of this cloth?	ফি অসিগী মমল কয়া পিরম্বগে	Phi asigî mamal kayâ pirambagê?
How much salt do you want?	নঙ থুম কয়া লৌনিঙই	Nang thum kayâ launingi?
How many boats are there?	অাসোমদা হি কয়া লৈবগে	Âsômdâ hi kayâ leibagê?
How many fowls have you bought?	নঙ য়েল কয়া লৈরক পগে	Nang yel kayâ leirak pagê?
How long will you be gone?	নঙ কয়া কুইরগা লাক্কদবগে	Nang kayâ kuiragâ lâkkadabagê?
How often shall I see you?	কয়ারক নঙবূ ঐনা য়েংগনি	Kayârak nangbû ainâ yenggani?
How many times have you been here?	নঙ কয়ারক অসিদা লাকই	Nang kayârak asidâ lâki?
How much shall I pay you a month?	নঙবূ থাদা রূপা কয়া পিগদবগে	Nangbû thâdâ rûpâ kayâ pigadabagê?
I am very hungry	ঐ চাক য়ামনা লামই	Ai châk yâmnâ lâmi.
Hush! you make a great noise	নঙ য়ামনা লাও খোংই তুমিন লৈয়ু	Nang yâmnâ lâo khôngi tumin leiyu.
I acknowledge my error	ঐ লাল্লে হাইবা য়ারে	Ai lâllê hâibâ yârê.
Do as I bid you	ঐগী হুকুম মতুং ইন্না তৌ	Aigî hukûm mattung innâ tau.
I will do as you bid me	নঙগী হুকুম মতুং ইন্না ঐ থবক তৌগনি	Nanggî hukum mattung innâ ai thabak taugani.
If there is none, go, buy, and bring	করিবুং লৈতরবদি চৎলু লৈরূ	Karisung leitarabadi chatlu leirû.
If I pronounce badly, tell me	বা সেংনা হাইদরবদি ঐ ঙোন্দা হাইয়ু	Wâ sengnâ hâidarabadi aingôndâ hâiyu.
If you do not pity me, who will?	নঙনা চানবিদরবদি কনানা ঐবূ চানবিগদবগে	Nangnâ chânbidarabadi kanânâ aibû chânbigadabagê?
Is he in the house?	মা য়ুমদা লৈব্রা	Mâ yumdâ leibrâ?
Who are in the boat?	হিদা কনা লৈবগে	Hidâ kanâ leibagê?

He feigns himself a fool in order to excite attention.	আঙাওব গুমনা তৌরবদি মি খৈবিকনা য়েংনগনি।	Angâoba gumnâ taurabadi mi khaibiknâ yengnagani.
Make what enquiries you please	বা পুম নমক অসি মমুত্তানা থিনবিয়ু	Wâ pum namak asi mamutânâ thinabiyu.
I shall be more pleased if you enquire	নঙনা বামুন্না থি নবিরবদি ঐ য়ামনা নুঙাইগনি	Nangnâ wâmunnâ thi narabadi ai yâmnâ nungâigani.
Go instantly	হৌজিক মক চৎখ্রো	Houjik mak chatkhrô.
He will work instead of his brother	ময়াম্মাগী মিহৎ সিন্দুনা মানা থবক তৌগনি	Mayâmmâgî mihut sindunâ mânâ thabak taugani.
Put it into the trunk	পোৎ অসি উপূদা থম্মু	Pôt asi upûdâ thammu.
Throw it into the water	ইসিংদা হুন্দোকউ	Isingdâ hundôku.
He came into the town	মা ইনফান্দা লাক্লে	Mâ inphândâ lâklê.
He inwardly proposed to kill me	মানা ঐবূ হাৎকে হাইদুনা মবুক্তা নিঙই	Mânâ aibû hâtkê haidunâ mabuktâ ningi.
Is this man irritable?	মি অসি সাওগনবা মিরা	Mi asi sâôganbâ mirâ ?
He is not irritable	মা সাওগনবা মি নত্তে	Mâ sâôganbâ mi nattê.
This man is a good man	মি অসি অফবা মিনি	Mi asi afabâ mini.
Is it a male elephant?	সামূ অসি লাবরা	Sâmû asi lâbrâ ?
Is there no well?	গোহা লৈতব্রা	Gôhâ leitabrâ?
There is, Sir	লৈ, সাহেব	Lei, sâhib.
Is there no candle?	খোইরু থাওমৈ লৈতব্রা	Khôiru thaumai leitabrâ?
Is it dry?	অসি অকংব্রা	Asi akangbrâ?
If dry, take it in	কংলবদি মনুংদা পূরকউ	Kanglabadi manungdâ pûraku.

English.	*Manipuri in Vernacular.*	*Manipuri in English Character.*
Is it true?	চুম্ব্রা।	Chumbrâ?
Where is the place for it?	অসিগী মফম কদাইনো	Asigî mapham kadâinô?
It is not true	অচুম্বা নত্তে	Achumbâ nattê.
It is right (proper), it is right (correct)	অরেপ্পনি, অচুম্বনি	Areppani, achumbani.
It thunders, it lightens	নোংখোংলে, নোংথাঙ কুপ্লে	Nôngkhônglê, nôngthâng kuplê.
The jackals carried off five fowls	লম হুইনা য়েল মঙা পূখ্রে	Lam huinâ yel mangâ pûkhrê.
Wash your jacket	ফুরিৎ অসি সু	Furit asi su.
He has just gone	মা হৌজিক চৎখ্রে	Mâ haujik chatkhrê.
He just escaped being drowned	ইসিংদা ইরাক নদুনা মা খজিকত দগী হিংলে	Isingdâ irâk nadunâ mâ khajikta dagî hinglê.
The enemy are just at hand	য়েকনবসিং নাক্তা লৈরে	Yeknabasing nâktâ leirê.
Keep this knife	সোরি অসি থম্মু	Sôri asi thammu.
Keep still	তুম্মিন লৈয়ু	Tummin leiyu.
Fasten it with a lock and key	অসি সো লোন সিল্লু	Asi sô lôn sillu.
That horse will kick you	সাগোন অসি নঙবু কাওগনি	Sâgôn asi nangbû kâôgani.
Do not kick the little dog	হুই অপিসা অসিবু খোঙনা কাওগনু	Hui apisâ asibû khôngnâ kâôganu.
He was killed in battle	মানা লানফমদা সিখ্রে	Mânâ lânphamdâ sikhrê.
This kind of plantain is the best	লফোই খৈবিক্তগী লফোই অসিগী জাৎনা হেন্না ফৈ।	Laphôi khaibiktagî laphôi asigî jâtnâ hennâ fai.
What kind of a man is he?	পুকচেন কমতৌবা মিনো।	Pukchen kamtaubâ minô?
There are animals of every kind	সা পুম্নমক জাৎ সুনা লৈ	Sâ pumnamak jât sunâ lei.
He is a very kind man	মি অদু য়ামনা থৌজানহৈবা মিনি	Mi adû yâmnâ thaujânhaibâ mini.

You will ruin the little knife	সোরি মচ্চা অদু মাঙগনি	Sôri machâ adu mânggani?
Do you know for a certainty?	নঙ লেপনমক খঙব্রা	Nang lepnamak khangbrâ?
Do you know how to make baskets?	নঙ থুম্মুক শাবা হৈব্রা	Nang thummuk shâbâ heibrâ?
Do you know this man?	নঙ মি অসি খঙব্রা	Nang mi asi khangbrâ?
I do not know how much there is	কয়ানো ঐ খঙদে	Kayânô ai khangdê.
The Assamese language is softer than the Bengali.	ময়াংলোন্দগী হেন্না তেখাওরোন্না ঙাঙবদা য়াম্না নৌই।	Mayânglôndagî hennâ tekhâorônnâ ngângbadâ yâmnâ naui.
Is it the language of the common people, or the language of the books?	হাইরিবা অসি চৎনরিবা লোল্লা লাইরিকী লোল্লা।	Hâiribâ asi chatnaribâ lôllâ lâirik-kî lôllâ?
Here is the last fowl	য়েল অসি অমত্তা ম ঙাই	Yel asi amattâ ma ngâi.
The man who came last is the best	কোন্না লাকপা মি অসিনা ক্বাইদগী ফৈ	Kônnâ lâkpâ mi asinâ kwâidagî fai.
Why do you come so late?	নঙ করি মরমনা অসুপ থেঙনা লাকপগে	Nang kari maramnâ asup thengnâ lâkpage.
Do not lie abed so late in the morning	অয়ুক অসুপ থেঙনা তুমগনু	Ayuk asup thengnâ tumganu.
I saw her lately	নুপি অদুবু উবা কুইদরী	Nupi adubû ubâ kuidarî.
You should lay up part of your money for future use.	নঙ্গী নরনবু নঙ্গী হাকতকতা খর থম্বনা ফৈ	Nanggî naranbu nanggî hâktaktâ khara thambanâ fai.
Where the roofs leaks, put on more thatch.	নোংয়ুবা মফম অসিদা ই খর কুপউ	Nôngyubâ mapham asidâ i khara kupu.
Do not lean upon the table	মেজগী মথক্তা ঙাগনু	Mejgî mathaktâ ngâganu.
You must learn to cook	নঙনা চাক থোংবা তম্মু	Nang châk thôngbâ tammu.
Do you wish to learn to read?	নঙ লাইরিক তম নিংব্রা	Nang lâirik tam ningbrâ?
How much shall I learn?	ঐনা কয়ামরম তম্বিগদবগে	Ainâ kayâmaram tam bigadabagê.
This is the least of all	মাসি ক্বাইদগী পিকই	Mâsi kwaidagî piki.

English.	*Manipuri in Vernacular.*	*Manipuri in English Character.*
Why did you go without my leave?	ঐনা সুতি থাদনা করিগী চৎপগে	Ainâ suti thâdanâ karigî chatpagê?
Go and bring the box which you left	নঙনা থনম্বা উপু অদু লৌরূ	Nanguâ thanambâ upu adu laurû.
I am not at leisure	ঐ সংদে	Ai sangde.
What is the length of this board?	উপাক অসি কয়া সাংবগে	Upâk asi kayâ sângbagê.
The more I pay him, the less he works	তলপতি অসুপ য়ামনা হেনগৎ লগা থবক্তি বাৎনা তৌরে।	Talabti asup yâmnâ hengat lagâ thabakti wâtnâ taurê.
Here are two loaves, I will take the lesser.	তল অনি লৈরিবা অসিদগী ঐ অপিসা লৌগে	Tal ani leiribâ asidagî ai apisâ laugê.
He was afraid lest he should break his leg.	মা মখোঙ তেককনি হাইদুনা কিরে	Ma makhông tekkani haidunâ kirê.
Let us go, let us bathe	ঐখোই চৎসি, ইরূজসি	Aikhôi chatsi, Irûjasi.
Let him come	মা লাকসনু	Ma lâksanu.
Let me see the knife	ঐবু সোরি য়েংহল্লু	Aibû sôri yenghallu.
You must not tell a lie	নঙ মিনম্বা বা হাইগনু	Nang minambâ wâ hâiganu.
It is light, it is not dark	নোংঙাল্লে, অমম্বা লৈত্রে	Nôngngâllê, amambâ leitrê.
This burden is light	পোৎ অসি য়াংই	Pôt asi yângi.
Light a lamp	থাওমৈ অমা থানগৎলু	Thâomai amâ thângatlu.
He is like the teacher	মা উঝা গুম্বা বৈরে	Mâ ujhâ gumbâ wairê.
He behaves like a king	মা নিংথৌগুমনা তৌরে	Mâ ningthaugumnâ taurê.
He swims like a duck	মা ঙানূগুমনা ই রোইরি	Mâ ngânûgumnâ i rôiri.
He is likely to be ruined	মা মহাম তারক কেতৌরে	Mâ mahâm târak kêtaurê.
Do likewise	অসুমনা তৌ	Asumnâ tau.

I want a little	ঐ খজিক্তং পামই	Ai khajiktang pâmi.
I understand it a little	ঐ খর খঙই	Ai khara khangi.
A fish cannot live out of water	ঙাদি ইসিং নত্তনা হিংবা ঙমদে	Ngâdi ising nattanâ hingbâ ngamdê.
Tell them to load the boat	হিদা পোং হাপউ হাইদুনা মাখোইদা হাইয়ু	Hidâ pôt hâpû hâidunâ mâkhôidâ hâiyu.
Lock the door	থোঙ সো লোল্লু	Thông sô lôllu.
The boy is lonesome	অঙাং মচ্চাদি মথন্না লৈরবদি বাই	Angâng machâdi mathannâ leirabadi wâi.
Look there	অসোমদা য়েংউ	Asômdâ yêngu.
What are you looking at?	নঙ করি য়েংবগে	Nang kari yengbagê ?
Bring me a long bamboo	বা অসাংবা অমদং ঐঙোন্দা পিয়ু	Wâ asângbâ amadang aingôndâ piyu.
It is ten yards long	অসি খুদুপ কুল সাংবনি	Asi khudup kul sângbani.
Build the house forty cubits long and thirty broad.	য়ুম খুদুপ নিফু সাংবা খুদুপ কুনথ্রা পাকপা অমদং সাও।	Yum khudup nifu sângbâ khudup kunthrâ pâkpâ amadang sâo.
I have lost my knife	ঐগী সোরি মাঙখ্রে	Aigî sôri mângkhrê.
This bank of the river is low	তুরেল মপাল অসোমদা নেমই	Turel mapâl asômdâ nemi.
The other side is still lower	অসোমদগী হেন্না বাংমা আসোমগী মপাল্না নেমই।	Asômdagî hennâ wângmâ âsômgî mapâlnâ nemi.
What is this made of?	অসি করিনা সাবগে	Asi karinâ sâbagê ?
Has the mail arrived to-day?	ঙসি ডাক থুংলব্রা থুংদরিব্রা	Ngasi dâk thunglabrâ thungdaribrâ ?
He stands in the main street	নিংথৌগী লমজাওদা লেপ্তুনা লৈ	Ningthaugî lamjâodâ lêptunâ lei.
I wish you to make me 20 mats	নঙ ঐগী ফক কুল সাও	Nang aigî phak kul sâo.
Make room for the gentleman to pass	সাহেবলুক চৎনবা লম্বি থৈদোকউ	Sâhebluk chatnabâ lambi theidôku.

English.	*Manipuri in Vernacular.*	*Manipuri in English Character.*
He makes him go	মানা মাবূ চৎহল্লি	Mânâ mâbû chathalli.
He makes him do it	মানা মাবূ থবক অসি তৌহল্লি	Mânâ mâbû thabak asi tauhalli.
What makes you sad?	নঙ্গী পুকনিঙদা করিণা বাবগে	Nanggî pukningdâ karinâ wâbagê?
This man is a religious man	মি অসি ধর্ম্ম চেনবা মিনি	Mi asi dharma chenbâ mini.
You should be mannerly	লেমনা তৌদুনা লৈগনী	Lemnâ taudunâ leiganî.
Take as many as you like	লৌনিঙবা অদুপ্কী মখৈ লৌ	Launingbâ adupkî makhai lau.
Do you want many men, or but few?	নঙ মি য়ামনা লৌগদ্রা, খজিক্তং লৌগদ্রা	Nang mi yâmnâ laugadrâ, khajiktang laugadrâ?
Mark what I say	ঐনা হাইবা বা অসি কাওগনু	Ainâ hâibâ wâ asi kâoganu.
I have made a mark	ঐনা খুদম পিখ্রে	Ainâ khudam pikhrê.
There is nothing the matter	করিসুং বা থোক্কদবা লৈতে	Karisung wâ thôkkadabâ leitê.
I must enquire into this matter	থবক অসিগী বা ঐ খোঙগুল্লিগে	Thabak asigî wâ ai khônggulligê.
May he come?	মা লাকপা য়াগদ্রা	Mâ lâkpâ yâgadrâ?
May I return home?	ঐগী য়ুমদা হনবা য়াগদ্রা	Aigî yumdâ hanbâ yâgadrâ?
May I arrive at happiness?	ঐ নুংঙাঈগদ্রা	Ai nungâîgadrâ?
I may not be here to-morrow	মফম অসিদা হয়েং ঐ লৈরোঈগব্রা খঙদ্রে	Mapham asidâ hayeng ai leirôîgabrâ khangdre.
What does this mean?	অসিগী অর্থ করিনো	Asigî artha karinô?
Have you measured this cloth?	নঙ ফি অসি খুদুপ ওল্লব্রা	Nang phi asi khudup ollabrâ?
It is merely this	মাদু মক্তনি	Mâdu maktani.
Place it in the middle	অসিময়াইদা থম্ম	Asi mayâidâ thammu.

From noon to midnight is twelve hours	নুমিৎ য়ুংবা দগী নোংঙ্গাই ফাওবা ঘন্টা তরানিথোইনি	Numit yungbâ dagî nôngyâi fâobâ ghantâ tarânithôini.
He stood in the midst of the multitude	মিয়াম্‌গী ময়াইদা মানা লেপ্‌লে	Miyâmgî mayâidâ mânâ leplê.
Ava is midway between Rangoon and Sadiya.	রেংগোঁগা সদিয়াগা মরক্তা অবা লৈ	Rongôngâ Sadiyâgâ maraktâ Avâ lei.
You might have gone	নঙ চৎলমগদবনি	Nang chatlamgadabani.
You might go now, if you wished	চৎনিঙলবদি হৌজিক নঙ চৎপা ঙমগনী	Chatninglabadi houjik nang chatpâ ngamganî.
Bring the milk	সংগোম পূরকউ	Sanggôm pûraku.
Milk the goats	হমেঙ সংগোম সুম্মু	Hameng sanggôm summu.
My mind is fixed	ঐগী পুকনিঙ লেপ্‌লে	Aigî pukning leplê.
Have you a mind to go?	নঙ চৎনিঙব্রা	Nang chatningbrâ ?
You do not mind me	নঙ ঐগী বা ইন্দে	Nang aigî wâ indê.
You have made a mistake	নঙসোইরে	Nang sôirê.
Why did you mix them together?	করিণা ময়াম অসি য়ান্নবগে	Karinâ mayâm asi yânnabagê?
His money is all gone	মাগী মরণ ঙমনমক তিংখ্রে	Mâgî maran ngamnamak tingkhrê.
Do not wait a moment	মিকুপ অমত্তা পনফদে	Mikup amattâ panfadê.
More is wanting	অসিদগী হেন্না লৌনিঙই	Asidagî hennâ launingi.
I want more than that	অসিদগী হেন্না পামই	Asidagî hennâ pâmi.
Can you give no more?	নঙ অসিদগী হেন্না পিবা ঙমওইদ্রা	Nang asidagî hennâ pibâ ngamoidrâ ?
There are more	মাসিদগী হেন্না লৈরী	Mâsidagî hennâ leirî.
You are more courageous than I	ঐঙোন্দগী নঙনা থবাই চাওবা হেল্লি	Aingôndagî nangnâ thawâi châobâ helli.
Come to-morrow morning	হয়েং অয়ুক লাকউ	Hayeng ayuk lâku.

English.	*Manipuri in Vernacular.*	*Manipuri in English Character.*
The butterfly is the most beautiful of all insects.	তিল কাঙ খৈবিক্তগী কুরাক্না হেন্না ফজৈ	Til kâng khaibiktagî kurâknâ hennâ fajei.
I am most happy to see you	নঙবূ উবদা ঐ য়ামনা হরাওই	Naugbû ubadâ ai yâmnâ harâoi.
I am mostly employed in writing	ঐগীদি লাঈরিক ইবা মক্তদা মতম হৌখ্রে	Aigîdi lâirik ibâ maktadâ matam haukhrê.
New York is at the mouth of a river	য়ুয়োর্ক কোনুংদি তুরেনগী মচিন্দা লৈ	New York kônungdi turengî machindâ lei.
Do not keep your mouth wide open	নঙগী নয়া কাথোকতুনা লৈগন্নু	Nanggî nayâ kâthôktunâ leigann.
Do not move those muskets	নোংমৈ পুমনমক অসি মফম অমদা হোং দোক্কন্নু	Nôngmai pumnamak asi mapham amadâ hông dôkkanu.
Move that trunk to the other side of the room.	উপূ অসি কা অসিগী ময়া আসোমদা থম্মু	Upû asi kâ asigî mayâ âsômdâ thammu.
A monkey is much larger than a mouse.	উচিদগী হেন্না য়োংনা চাওই	Uchidagî hennâ yôngnâ châoi.
I am much afraid	ঐ য়ামনা কিরে	Ai yâmnâ kirê.
There is much talk, you must remain quiet.	য়ামনা নিনখোংই তুমিন লৈয়ু	Yâmnâ ninkhôngi tumin leiyu.
Must I call him	ঐবূ মাবূ কৌরূ হাইব্রা	Aibû mâbû kaurû hâibrâ.
He must come	মা তংঙাই ফদনা লাকপা থোকই	Mâ tang ngâi fadanâ lâkpâ thôki.
My mother calls me, I must go	ইমানা ঐবূ কৌরে, চৎপা থোকলে	Imânâ aibû kaurê, chatpâ thôklê.
I will do it myself	ঐ ইথন্না তৌগে	Ai ithannâ taugê.
Drive a nail into that post	য়ুম্বি অসিদা য়োৎপি য়ৈসিল্লু	Yumbi asidâ yôtpi yeisillu.
It would be well if you should cut your finger nails.	নঙগী খুজিন ককূলবদি ফগনী	Nangî khûjin kaklabadi faganî.

Tell that boy not to come here naked	অঙাং মচ্চাদা হাইয়ু ফি সেৎস্না লাক্কনু	Angâng machâdâ hâiyu phi settanâ lâkkanu.
What is your name?	নঙগী নমিং করি কৌবগে	Nanggî naming kari kaubagê ?
It is human nature to resent injuries	মি ওঈবগী হৌনবনি মংসক তানবা হাইবসি	Mi oibagi haunabani mangsak tânbâ hâibasi.
His house is near	মাগী ময়ুম নকই	Mâgî mayum naki.
He is nearly dead	মা সিগে তৌরে	Mâ sigê taurê.
This is neat writing	লাঈরিক ইবা অসি ময়েক সেংই	Lâîrik ibâ asi mayek sengi.
It is necessary to have laws	লাঈরিক্না হাইবা ৱায়েল সোইদনা চৎপা থোকই।	Lâîriknâ hâibâ wâyel sôidunâ chatpâ thôki.
They need an overseer	মা খোইগী মথক্তা মিয়েং অমা হাপ্পা থোকই।	Mâ khôigî mathaktâ miyeng amâ hâp-pâ thôki.
You need not go	নঙ চৎকদবা লৈতে	Nang chatkadabâ leitê.
We are very needy	ঐখোই য়ামনা নঙবা মিনি	Aikhôi yâmnâ nangbâ mini.
An idol can neither speak, see, nor hear.	লাঈগী মূর্ত্তিদি ৱা ঙাঙদে উদে তাদে	Liâgî mûrtidi wâ ngângdê udê tâdê.
The Miris remain neutral	মিরি লোকতি কনাগী মিচঙসুং ওঈদে	Miri lôkti kanâgî michangsung oi-dê.
They never fight	মাখোইদি করিগুম্বদসুং লাল সোকনবা তৌদে।	Mâkhôidi karigumbadasung lâl sôknabâ taudê.
Nevertheless, they will not consent to be slaves.	তোইগুম্বসুং মাখোই করিগুম্বদসুং মিনাঈ ওঈয়ু হাইবা য়াদে।	Tauigumbasung mâkhôi karigumba-dasung minâî oîyu hâibâ yâdê.
Never mind, it is of no consequence	করি থৌলৈতে নিংসাথিবা তৌগনু !	Kari thauleite ningsâthibâ tauganu.
That man is a new comer.	মি অসি নৌনা লাকপনি	Mi asi naunâ lâkpani.

English.	*Manipuri in Vernacular.*	*Manipuri in English Character.*
Who is the next ?	মাগী মথংদা কনানো	Mâgî mathangdâ kanânô ?
That tree will bear fruit next year	উপাল অসি ওল্লককদবা চহিদা মহৈ পালগনী।	Upâl asi ollakkadabâ chahidâ mâhei pâlganî.
The Khamtis will come next year	খামটিদি ওল্লক কদবা চহিদা লাক্কনী	Khâmtidi ollakkadabâ chahidâ lâk-kanî.
They are already nigh	মাখোইদি হৌজিকতি নক্লে	Mâkhôidi houjikti naklê.
Let no one come nigh the house in the night.	অহিংদা য়ুমগী মনাক্তা কনাসুং লাকহলগনু	Ahingdâ yumgî manâktâ kanâsung lâk-halganu.
No, Sir, it is not	সাহেব মাঈ, মাসি নত্তে	Sâheb mâî, mâsi nattê.
Make no noise	লাও খোংগনু	Lâo khônganu.
What noise is that?	মাসি করি মখোন্নো	Mâsi kari makhônnô ?
None of us can tell	ঐখোই অমত্তসুং হাইবা ঙমদে	Aikhôi amattasung hâibâ ngamde.
There are none. There is nothing	লৈতে, অমত্তসুং লৈতে	Leitê, amattasung leitê.
Give dinner at noon	নুমিৎ য়ুংবা মতমদা চাক পিজৌ	Numit yungbâ matamdâ châk pijau.
Which way is north ?	মাইগৈ কদোমদা অৱাংনো	Mâigei kadômdâ awângnô ?
He has not arrived	মা থুংদরি	Mâ thungdari.
It is not good	মাসি অফবা নত্তে	Mâsi aphabâ nattê.
I wish for nothing	ঐকরি অমত্তসুং নিংবা লৈতে	Aikari amattasung ningbâ leitê.
There is nothing more to be done	অমুক করিসুং তৌগদবা লৈতি	Amuk karisung taugadabâ leitê.
Have you no oars ?	নঙ্গী নৌ লৈত্রা	Nanggî nau leitrâ ?
Obey your parents	নমা নপাগী ৱা তাগদবা ওঈ	Namâ napâgî wâ tâgadabâ oî.
He is an officer of the king	মানা নিংথৌগী ফমনাঈবা ওঈরী	Mânâ ningthaugî phamnâîbâ oîrî.

The law of God	লাঈগী বায়েল	Lâigî wâyel.
By order of the Rája	নিংথৌগী য়াথংদগী	Ningthaugî yâthangdagî.
A piece of paper	চে মচেৎ	Che machet.
He died of fever	মা অরুম হৌঃদুনা সিরে	Mâ arum haudunâ sirê.
The best of the three	অহুমক্তগী হেন্না ফবা	Ahummaktagî hennâ fabâ.
Get off that horse	সাগোন মথক্তগী কুম্মু	Sâgôn mathaktagî kummu.
Have you been there often, or only once?	মাদুদা নঙ কয়ারক চৎলূবগে অমক্তা চৎলূব্রা	Mâdudâ naug kayârak chatlûbagê amaktâ chatlûbrâ?
Oh! I have dropped a rupee into the water.	ইহে! ঐগী রূপা অমা ইসিংদা তাখ্রে	Ihê! aigî rûpâ amâ isingdâ tâkhrê.
Have you put oil in the lamps?	নঙ মিংসেন থাওমৈদা থাও হাপলম্ব্রা	Nang mingsen thâomaidâ thâo hâplambrâ?
Is it a new boat, or an old one?	হি অসি অহনব্রা, অমনব্রা	Hi asi ahanbrâ, amanbrâ?
I once was young, and now am old	হান্নদি অঙাং ওঈরমই হৌজিক্তি হন্নুবা ওঈরে।	Hânnadi angâng oîrami haujikti hannubâ oîrê.
Is there a man on the hill?	চিঙ মথক্তা মি অমা লৈব্রা	Ching mathaktâ mi amâ leibrâ?
Place it on the table	মেজ্গী মথক্তা থম্মু	Mejgî mathaktâ thammu.
Step on the board, and pass over	উপাক মথক্তা লান্দুনা চৎখো	Upâk mathaktâ lândunâ chatkhô.
One jacket is white, the other is black	ফুরিৎ অমনা অঙৌবনি অমদি অমূবনি	Furit amanâ angaubani amadi amûbani.
He went one way, I another	মানা লম্বি অমদা চৎখি ঐনা লম্বি অমদা চৎলি।	Mânâ lambi amadâ chatkhi ainâ lambi amadâ chatli.
No one understands it	কনাসুং মাসি খঙদে	Kanâsung mâsi khangdê.
There is but one God	লাঈ অমত্তনি	Lâî amattani.

English.	*Manipuri in Vernacular.*	*Manipuri in English Character.*
Why do you quarrel with one another?	নহৈ নহৈ কদৌডুনা খৎনবগে	Nahei nahei kadaudunâ khatnabagê?
Open the door, open that chest	থোঙ হাংদোকউ, উপু হাংদোকউ	Thông hângdôku, upu hângdôku.
I have had no opportunity to speak with him.	মাগা বা ঙাঙনগদবা খুদোং চাদ্রে	Mâgâ wâ ngângnagadabâ khudông châdrê.
His house is opposite to mine	মাগী য়ুমগা ঐগী য়ুমগা মাইয়োকনৈ	Mâgî yumgâ aigî yumgâ mâiyôknei.
Good or bad, bring whatever there is	অফবা ওঈরবসুং ফত্তবা ওঈরবসুং অরৈবা মখৈ পূরকউ।	Afabâ oîrabasung fattabâ oîrabasung areibâ makhai pûraku.
Go out and shoot a deer and a wild hog.	মপান্থোকতুনা সজি অমা লমওক অমা নোংমৈনা কাপউ।	Mapânthôktunâ saji amâ lamôk amâ nôngmeinâ kâpu.
He sends a royal order throughout the country.	মানা নিংথৌগী য়াথং লৈপাক পুম্নমকতা চেন্থোকই।	Mânâ ningthaugî yâthang leipâk pumnamaktâ chenthôki.
He went in order to die	মা সিগে হাইবগী দমক চৎখ্রে	Mâ sigê hâibagî damak chatkhrê.
He weeps in order to excite pity	মিনা চানবিসনু হাইবগী কপই	Minâ chânbisanu hâibagî kapi.
The soldiers are orderly	সিফাইসিং বায়েল কাইদনা লৈ	Siphâising wâyel kâidanâ lei.
He ordinarily comes earlier	মানা সিনজাংওঈনা ঙন্না লাকই	Mânâ sinjângoînâ ngannâ lâki.
Otherwise I would dismiss him	মাসি নত্তরবদি মাবু ঐনা তোকহনগে	Mâsi nattarabadi mâbû ainâ tôkhangê.
He ought to come earlier	মা খর ঙন্না থুংল গদবনি	Mâ khara ngannâ thungla gadabani.
Is this our boat?	হি অসি ঐখোইগীরা	Hi asi aikhôigîrâ?
Bale out the water	ইসিং সিৎ তোকউ	Ising sit tôku.
Pull out that drawer	মেজগী উপু সৎ তোকউ	Mejgî upû sat tóku.
It was taken out of the ship	হি ডিংগা দগি মাসি লৌথোকখ্রে	Hi dingâ dagi mâsi lauthôkkhrê.
He stands outside of the house	য়ুম্গী মপাল্দা লেপ্তুনা লৈ	Yumgî mapâldâ leptunâ lei,

Do not turn over that pail of water	ইসিং বাল্টি অসি হৈদোককনু	Ising bâlti asi heidôkkanu.
Will the goats leap over this fence?	হমেঙসিং অসি সনবল চোংবা ঙমগদ্রা	Hamengsing asi sanbal chôngbâ ngamgadrâ ?
I have bought a pair of doves	লম খুনূ পু অমদং ঐনা লৈরূই	Lam khunû pu amadang ainâ leirûi.
Place them parallel	পুম নমক অসি চপমান্ননা পরেংসানা থম্মু	Pum namak asi chapmânnanâ parengsânâ thammu.
Do you give him a part of your plantains?	লফোই সরুক অমদং মাঙোন্দা পিরম্ব্রা	Laphôi saruk amadang mângôndâ pirambrâ ?
He passed by me	মানা ঐবূ লেংথৈনদুনা চৎখি	Mânâ âibû lengtheinadunâ chatkhi.
It is past	হৌখ্রে	Houkhrê.
Perhaps he will come	মা লাকপসুং য়াই লাক্তবসুং য়াই	Mâ lâkpasung yâi lâktabasung yâi.
He answered me very pertly	মানা মচোক মপাক নাইদনা খুম্মি	Mânâ machôk mapâk nâidanâ khummi.
What is this the picture of?	অসি করি পোৎকী নোকসান্নো	Asi kari pôtkî nôksânnô.
Have pity, my lord	ইবুংঙোনা থৌজানবিগনী	Ibungônâ thaujânbiganî.
I am fond of plantains	ঐ লফোই চাবা পামই	Ai laphôi châbâ pâmi.
He says he will come positively	মানা হাইবা সোইদনা লাক্কনী	Mânâ hâibâ sôidanâ lâkkanî.
Pour some hot water from the tea kettle.	চা-থমলিবদগী ইসিং অসাবা হৈথৌ	Châ-thamlibadagî ising asâbâ heithau.
Pour out the tea	চা হৈথৌ	Châ heithau.
Do not praise him	মাবূ থাগৎকনু	Mâbû thâgatkanu.
I give him this as a present	পোৎ অসি নঙোন্দা বকসিস পিবনি	Pôt asi nangôngdâ baksis pibani.
What is the price of that?	সিগী মমল কয়ানো	Asigî mamal kayânô ?

English.	*Manipuri in Vernacular.*	*Manipuri in English Character.*
I will tell you privately	নঙবু ঐনা চিক্না হাইগে	Nangbû ainâ chiknâ hâigê.
Probably you will meet him	নঙগা মাগা ওকনবা য়াই	Nanggâ mâgâ oknabâ yâi.
It is not proper to work on the sabbath.	নোংমাইজিঙ নুমিত্তা থবক তৌবা হৌনদে	Nôngmâijing numittâ thabak taubâ haunadê.
This is a very proud man	মি অসি য়ামনা থোইবা মিনি	Mi asi yâmnâ thôibâ mini.
He acts very prudently	মা য়ামনা চেকসিন্না থবক তৌই	Mâ yâmnâ cheksinnâ thabak taui.
Pull up the weeds, and throw them away.	নাপি ফোইদোকতুনা হনজেকউ	Nâpi phôidôktunâ hunjeku.
Shall I put it in the earthen pot?	ইসিং পুন্দা অসি থমগদ্রা	Ising pundâ asi thamgadrâ?
Put it in the sun	নুংসাদা অসি থম্মু	Nungsâdâ asi thammu.
Put the tea-cups and saucers on the table.	পুখমগা খুজাইগা মেজদা থম্মু	Pukhamgâ khujâigâ mejdâ thammu.
Put on the child's hat	অঙাং মচাগী মকোকতা তুপি উপ্‌পিয়ু	Angâng machâgî makôktâ tupi uppiyu.
What is the cause of the quarrel?	খৎনরিবা অসি মরম করিগীনো	Khatnaribâ asi maram karigînô?
Here is a quarter	অসি পবা অমনি	Asi pawâ amani.
Come quickly	থুনা লাকউ	Thûnâ lâku.
He is quite crazy	মাদি অঙাও বনি	Mâdi angâo bani.
It will rain soon	থুনা নোংচুগনী	Thûnâ nôngchuganî.
He ran away	মা চেনখ্রে	Mâ chenkhrê.
He ran as fast as he could	মানা ঙম্বা মখৈ চেনখ্রে	Mânâ ngambâ makhai chenkhrê.

The cat has caught a rat	হৌদোঙনা উচি অমা ফারে	Haudôngnâ uchi amâ phârê.
Will you cut a bundle of ratans ?	লি মপুন অমা যান বিগেরা	Li mapun amâ yân bigerâ ?
I would rather go to Ava than Calcutta	কলকতা চৎপদগী হেন্না অবা চৎপা পামই	Calcutta chatpadagî hennâ Avâ chatpâ pâmi.
I do not like to eat raw onions	তিলৌ অহিংবদি ঐ চানিঙদে	Tilau ahingbadi ai châningdê.
Have everything in readiness	পোৎ পুমনমক থৌরাঙ তৌ	Pôt pumnamak thaurâng tau.
We are not ready, Sir	ঐখোই থৌরাঙ তৌদে, সাহেব	Aikhôi thaurâng taude, sâheb.
What is the reason ?	করি মরম্না	Kari maramnâ ?
I have reckoned up the account	ঐ হিসাব তৌরে	Ai hisâb taurê.
Bring some reeds to weave a mat	ফক সানবা মচাক পুরকউ	Phak sânabâ machâk puraku.
He lives without religion	ধর্ম্মদি তৌদনা হিংদুনা লৈরি	Dharmadi taudanâ hingdunâ leiri.
Let it remain	লৈসনু	Leisanu.
I remember my old freinds	ঐগী মরূপ কুইখরবা নিঙসিংলুই	Aigî marup kuikharabâ ningsinglui.
You must repair the roof	য়ুম থক নিঙথিনা ফোৎলু	Yum thak ningthinâ fôtlu.
I respect the teacher	উঝাবু নোন্না রুকনা ঐ তৌই	Ujhâbu nônnâ rukanâ ai taui.
He has returned	মা হল্লকলে	Mâ hallaklê.
Turn to the right hand	য়েৎ লোমদা লৈয়ু	Yet lômdâ leiyu.
That is right	মাসি চুমই	Mâsi chumi.
Ring the bell	পুঙজা য়েয়ু	Pungjâ yeiyu.
These mangoes are not ripe	হৈনৌ অসি মুন্দে	Heinau asi mundê.
Rise up, the sun has risen	হৌগৎলু, নুমিৎ থোকলে	Haugatlu, numit thôklê.
Where does the road lead ?	লম্বি অসি কদাই য়ৌবগে	Lambi asi kadâi yaubagê ?
Do not let the boat rock	হি অসি লোইহন গনু	Hi asi lôihan ganu.

English.	*Manipuri in Vernacular.*	*Manipuri in English Character.*
Roll up the bed curtains	কাঙখল হাঈগৎলু	Kângkhal hâîgatlu.
The stone rolls, because it is round	মুঙডুম ওঈডুনা ওল্লি	Nungdum oîdunâ olli.
It is in that room	মাসি কা অসিদা লৈ	Mâsi kâ asidâ lei.
Let us fix a rope round that rock, and pull it over.	ঐখোই থৌরিনা মুঙ পুন্দুনা হুন্দনসি	Aikhôi thaurinâ nung purdunâ hundanasi.
The peaches are all rotten	চুমবরৈ ঙম নমক পুম্লে	Chumbarai ngam namak pumlê.
Set these trees in a row	উপাল পুম নমক অসি পরেংসানা থাও	Upâl pum namak asi parengsânâ thâo.
Row on, row on	হি হোল্লু হোল্লু	Hi hôllu hôllu.
I do not understand rowing a boat	ঐ হি হোনবা হৈতে	Ai hi hônbâ heitê.
Is it not wicked to drink rum ?	য়ু থকপা ফত্তবা নত্তরা	Yu thakpâ fattabâ nattarâ?
Run quick, and fetch it	থুনা চেন্দুনা পুরকউ	Thûnâ chendunâ pûraku.
I did it for his sake	মাগী মরমগীদমক ঐনা তৌরে	Mâgî maramgîdamak ainâ taurê.
He does it for the sake of money	রূপাগী মরমগীদমক মানা তৌরিবা সিনি	Rûpâgî maramgîdamak mânâ tauribâ sini.
Show me a sample of the salt	থুমগী মওঙ ঐবু য়েং হল্লু	Thumgî maong aibû yeng hallu.
Is it all the same?	অমহা নত্তরা	Amahâ nattarâ?
What do you say?	নঙ করি হাইবগে	Nang kari hâibagê?
One side of these scales is too heavy	পাবোৎ অসি অসোমদা হেন্না লুম থরে	Pâbôt asi asômdâ hennâ lum tharê.
The books are all scattered about	লাঈরিক কিতাপ পুম নমক চাইথোক তুনা লৈ	Lâîrik kitâp pun namak châithôk tunâ lei.
It is now the rainy season	হৌজিক নোংজু থানি	Houjik nôngju thâni.

I have searched, but cannot find it	ঐনা য়ামনা থিববূ ফংদে	Ainâ yâmnâ thibabû phangdê.
Do you not see it?	নঙ অসি উদব্রা	Nang asi udabrâ?
See, if this word is in the dictionary	বা অসি লোন হন্দোকপা লাঈরিকতা লৈব্রা য়েংউ।	Wâ asi lôn handôkpâ lâiriktâ leibrâ yengu.
Plant these seeds in the garden	মরু অসি ইংখোন্দা থাও	Maru asi ingkhôndâ thâo.
What are you seeking?	নঙ করি থিবগে	Nang kari thibagê?
I have seen the sun shine	নুমিৎ ঙালবা উই	Numit ngâlbâ ui.
I have not seen it	ঐ অসি উদে	Ai asi udê.
How do you sell those goods?	পোৎ অসি নঙ কমতৌনা য়োল্লিবগে	Pôt asi nang kamtaunâ yôllibagê?
Shall I send a pony?	সাগোন অমদং থিল্লকউ হাইব্রা	Sâgôn amadang thillaku hâibrâ?
I will thank you to send me several	চান বিরবদি খর থিন বিরকউ	Chân birabadi khara thin biraku.
Set the table	মেজ থাও	Mej thâo.
Dig a hole and set out that tree.	কোম অমা তৌদুনা উপাল অসি থাও	Kôm amâ taudunâ upâl asi thâo.
Shake off some plums	চকপা হৈগ্রু নিকতুনা তাহল্লু	Chakpâ heigru niktunâ tâhallu.
Shall I burn it?	অসি ঐবূ মৈ থাদোকউ হাইব্রা	Asi aibû mai thâdôku hâibrâ?
The stream is so shallow, the boat cannot come.	তুরেল ইসিং ময়েং য়ামনা তাদুনা হি কাবা য়াদরে।	Turel ising mayeng yâmnâ tâdunâ hi kâbâ yâdarê.
She wears a shawl	নুপি অসি শালগী ইন্নফি ইল্লি	Nupi asi shâlgî innaphi illi.
Sit in the shade of this tree	উ অসিগী উরুমদা ফম্মু	U asigî urûmdâ phammu.
It shines like the sun	নুমিৎ কুমনা ঙাল্লি	Numit kumnâ ngâlli.
Three ships have arrived	হি ডিংগা অহুম থুংলে	Hi dinggâ ahum thunglê.
This bamboo is too short	বা অসি য়াম্না তেল্লি	Wâ asi yâmnâ telli.
I should go to-day, if I were ready	থৌরাঙ তৌরম লবদি ঐ ঙসি চৎকা দবনি	Thaurâng tauram labadi ai ngasi chatkâ dabani.

English.	*Manipuri in Vernacular.*	*Manipuri in English Character.*
Why should I steal?	মরম করিণা ঐ হুরান গদবগে	Maram karinâ ai hurân gadabagê ?
Show me the road	ঐবু লম্বি তাকউ	Aibû lambi tâku.
The door is shut	থোঙ থিংলী	Thông thinglî.
Shut the door	থোঙ থিংউ	Thông thingu.
Shut your book, and sit down	লাঈরিক য়োম্সিন্দুনা ফমউ	Lâirik yômsindunâ famu.
It is on this side	অসোমদা লৈ	Asômdâ lei.
It is six months since he died	মা সিখীবা থা তরুক শুরে	Mâ sikhîbâ thâ taruk surê.
This is my elder sister	মাসি ইচেমনি	Mâsi ichemni.
I have two younger sisters	ঐগী ইচন অনি লৈ	Aigî ichan ani lei.
Sit down	ফমউ	Famu.
Do not sit on the steps	নঙ সিরীদা ফমগনু	Nang sirîdâ famganu.
Place them slanting	পুম নমক ঙামনা থমউ	Pum namak ngâmnâ thamu.
He goes very slow	মা য়ামনা তপনা চৎলি	Mâ yâmnâ tapnâ chatli.
Where did you put the small spoon?	খৈরোই অপিসা কদাইদা থম্বগে	Khairôi apisâ kadâidâ thambagê ?
Do not let there be any smoke	য়েংউ মৈখু খুহনগনু	Yengu maikhu khûhanganu.
Why do you stay so long?	নঙ মরম করিণা অসুপ থিন্না লৈবগে	Nang maram karinâ asup thinnâ leibagê ?
You must not do so	নঙ অসুমনা তৌগনু	Nang asumnâ tauganu.
He has stopped up the road so that I cannot get along.	মানা অদুম্না লম্বি থিংদুনা ঐ চৎপা ঙমদ্রে	Mâuâ adumnâ lambi thingdunâ ai chatpâ ngamdrê.
If so, he is a bad man	অদু ওঈরবদি মাদি ফত্তবা মিনি	Adu oîrabadi mâdi fattabâ mini.
Some are good, some bad	খর ফৈ, খর ফত্তে	Khara fai, khara fattê.

It is at some considerable distance from here.	অসিদগী য়ামনা থাপই	Asidagî yâmnâ thâpi.
Some one has stolen it	মি অমনা পোৎ অসি হুরমই	Mi amanâ pôt asi hurami.
Somebody has been here	মি অমনা অসিদা লৈরমই	Mi amanâ asidâ leirami.
Something must be done	খর তৌগদবা ওঈ	Khara taugadabâ oî.
How can he do it	মাবূ করমতৌনা তৌগদবগে	Mâbû karamtaunâ taugadabagê.
He comes sometimes	মা করিগুম্বদা লাকই	Mâ kârigumbadâ lâki.
Sometimes he stops at his house	করি করিগুম্বদা মানা মাগী ময়ুমদা লৈ	Kari karigumbadâ mânâ mâgî mayumdâ lei.
He is somewhat rude	মা মচৎ খর নাঈদে	Mâ machat khara nâidê.
He must be somewhere on the hill	মা চিঙ থক্তা মফম অমদা লৈরমগনী	Mâ ching thaktâ mafam amadâ leiramganî.
It will soon be dark	খর লৈরগা মমগনী	Khara leiragâ mamganî.
I am sorry I have broken your umbrella.	নঙগী পে তেকহন্দুনা ঐ নুংঙাইত্রে	Nanggî pê tekhandunâ ai nungâitrê.
Of what sort is it?	করম্বা মওঙনো	Karambâ maongnô ?
How many sorts of rice are there?	চেঙ মরম কয়া লৈবগে	Cheng maram kayâ leibagê ?
Sort out these potatoes	আলূ পুম নমক্ অসি মখল মখল খল্লু	Âlû pum namak asi makhal makhal khallu.
Do you hear the sound of cannon?	নঙ তোপকী মখোন্তাব্রা	Nang tôpkî makhôntâbrâ ?
They travelled southward	মাখোইনা মখারোমদা লংফৈ চৎখ্রে	Mâkhôinâ makhârômdâ langfai chatkhrê.
Do the Assamese speak in this way?	তেখাওগী মিদি অসুমনা বা হাইবা হৌনব্রা	Tekhâogî midi asumnâ wâ hâibâ haunabrâ ?
Can you speak English?	নঙ ফিরিংগিগী লোন হৈব্রা	Nang firinggigî lôn haibrâ ?
I can speak a little	ঐ খরদি থোকই	Ai kharadi thôki.

English.	*Manipuri in Vernacular.*	*Manipuri in English Character.*
Split that bamboo	ৱা অসি খাইদোকউ	Wâ asi khâidôku.
The board is split	উপাক অসি চিংখাইরে	Upâk asi chingkhâirê.
Spread the sail	পাল তিংথোকউ	Pâl tingthôku.
Will you make me a square table?	ঐগী দমক চিথেক মরি নাঈনা মেজ অমদং চনবিগেরা।	Aigî damak chithek mari nâînâ mej amadang chaubigerâ?
Do not stay long	য়ামনা কুঈনা লৈগনু	Yâmnâ kuînâ leiganu.
Can you steer a boat?	নঙ হিনাও সাবা হৈব্রা	Nang hinâo sâbâ haibrâ?
He is still engaged in study	হৌজিক ফাওবা তমদুনা লৈ	Houjik fâobâ tamdunâ lei.
If that bumble-bee stings you, it will be very painful.	খোঈনা চিক্লবদি য়ামনা নাগনী	Khôînâ chiklabadi yâmnâ nâganî.
Stop a moment	খর লৈয়ু	Khara leiyu.
Why are you stopping?	নঙ করি মরমনা লেপ্তুনা লৈরীবগে	Nang kari maramnâ leptunâ leirîbagê?
Strain this milk through a cloth	সংগোম অসি ফিদা চুমথোকউ	Sanggôm asi fidâ chumthôku.
Stretch out your hand	নখুৎ তিংথোকউ	Nakhut tingthôku.
Strike out the gong	সেনবুঙ য়ৈয়ু	Senbung yaiyu.
Such language is very vile	ৱা অসি য়ামনা থিদা	Wâ asi yâmnâ thidâ.
I cannot employ such a man	অসি গুম্বা মিদা ঐ থবক পিবা ঙমলোঈ	Asi gumbâ midâ ai thabak pibâ ngamlôî.
How can you ask such a price?	মমন অসুপ কন্না করম হাইবগে	Maman asup kannâ karam hâibagê?
It is not sufficient	ওকতরী	Oktarî.
Sweep this room clean	কা অসি সেংনা সিত্তোকউ	Kâ asi sengnâ sittôku.

Does the water run swiftly ?	ইসিং অসি য়ামনা চেনব্রা	Ising asi yâmnâ chenbrâ ?
A steam-boat goes very swiftly	মৈগী হি য়ামনা থুনা চৎলি	Maigî hi yâmnâ thûnâ chatli.
Take out the knives and forks	সোরি কান্টা লৌথোকউ	Sôri kântâ lauthôku.
Which will you take, this or that ?	অনিমক অসিদগী করম্বা লৌগেগে, অসিরা আসিরা।	Animak asidagî karambâ laugêgê, asirâ âsirâ ?
Who has taken the axe ?	সিঙজঙ কনানা পুখরবগে	Singjang kanânâ pukharabagê ?
Dot not talk	বা ঙাঙগনু	Wâ gnângganu.
That is a tall man	মাসি অবাংবা মিনি	Mâsi awângbâ mini.
Why do you go with your hair tangled ?	নঙ করিণা নসম হাত্তোক তবগে	Nang karinâ nasam hâttôk tabagê.
Prepare and give tea	চা সেমদুনা পিয়ু	Châ semdunâ piyu.
The teacher says do not do it	উঝানা হাই, তৌগনু	Ujhânâ hâi, tauganu.
Do not tell anybody	কনাদসুং হাইগনু	Kanâdasung hâiganu.
This is larger than that	আসিদগী অসিনা হেন্না চাওই	Âsidagî asinâ hennâ châoi.
I thank you	য়ামনা নুংঙাইরে	Yâmnâ nungâirê.
I tell you that he is a great deceiver	ঐনা হাইবদি মাদি য়ামনা নমহৎকনবা মিনি	Ainâ hâibadi mâdi yâmnâ namhat kanbâ mini.
He promised that he would pay me	ঐগী ফংগদবা লৈবা অদু পিগনী হাইদুনা য়ারমলে।	Aigî fangadabâ leibâ adu piganî hâidunâ yâramlê.
How many loads of thatch have you brought to-day ?	নঙ ঙসী ই পোৎ কয়া পূরক পগে	Nang ngasî i pôt kayâ pûrak pagê ?
Their pride will ruin them	নাপল তৌবা মরমনা মাখোই মাঙগনী	Nâpal taubâ maramnâ mâkhôi mângganî.
They think too highly of themselves	মাখোই অসি মথন্ননা অচৌবা মিনি হাইদুনা নিঙই।	Mâkhôi asi mathannanâ achaubâ mini hâidunâ ningi.

English.	*Manipuri in Vernacular.*	*Manipuri in English Character.*
Then I must go	অদুনা ঐ চৎপা থোকই	Adunâ ai chatpâ thôki.
Do not go there	মাদুদা চৎকনু	Mâdudâ chatkanu.
There is a tiger there	আসোমদা কৈ লৈ	Âsômdâ kai lei.
How many elephants are there?	আসোমদা সামু কয়া লৈবগে	Âsômdâ sâmu kayâ leibagê?
There are four or five	মরি মঙা লৈ	Mari mangâ lei.
Thereupon he departed	মাদুগী মত্তুংদা চৎখ্রে	Mâdugi mattungdâ chatkhrê.
I was engaged yesterday, therefore I could not come.	ঙরাং ঐগী থবক লৈরদুনা অদুনা লাক্পা ঙমদ্রে।	Ngarâng aigi thabak leiradunâ adunâ lâkpâ ngamdrê.
These things are useless	পোৎ অসি করি থবক লৈতে	Pôt asi kari thabak leitê.
These are better than those	পোৎ অসি আসিদগী হেন্নাফৈ	Pôt asi âsidagi hennâfai.
I did not say so, they said it	ঐ অসুম হাইদে, মাখোইনা হাইবনি	Ai asum hâidê, mâkhôinâ hâibani.
Where do you think they have gone?	মাখোই কদাইদা চৎখিবগে নঙ খঙহৌব্রা	Mâkhôi Kadâidâ chatkhibagê nang khanghaubrâ?
What do you think?	নঙ করি খল্লিবগে	Nang kari khallibagê?
What do you call this?	মাসি করি হাইবগে	Mâsi kari hâibagê?
Though he fell from a high tree, he was not killed.	উ অৱাংবদগী তাই হাইববু মাসিদে	U awângbadagidi tâi hâibabu mâsidê.
They conquered, though they lost a thousand men.	মাখোইনদি ঙমই হাইববু মাখোইগী মি লিসিং অমা মাংলে।	Mâkôinadi ngami hâibabû mâkôigi mi lising amâ mânglê.
I thought he had gone	মা চৎখ্রে হাইনা নিংলে	Mâ chatkhrê hâinâ ninglê.
He has travelled through China	মানা খাগি লৈপাক পুম নমক থুংনা চৎলি	Mânâ khâgi leipâk pum namak thungnâ chatli.

The news spread througout the kingdom.	লৈপাক পুম নমক বা পাও সিন থুংলে	Leipâk pum namak wâ pâo sin thunglê.
Throw out this water	ইসিং অসি হুনজেকউ	Ising asi hunjeku.
Thus he said	মরম অসুমনা হাইবনি	Maram asumnâ hâibani.
By conducting himself thus he has destroyed his reputation.	অসুম তৌনা চৎপা অসিনা মাগী মিংচৎপা মাঙবনি।	Asum tannâ chatpâ asinâ mâgi mingchatpâ mângbani.
Draw this tight	মাসি কন্না চিংউ	Mâsi kannâ chingu.
He did not come till noon	নুমিৎ যুংবা ফাওবা মা লাকত্রে	Numit yungbâ fâobâ mâ lâktrê.
At the time of going another ship arrived.	চৎলাঈদমদা ঝহাজ অতোপ্পা অমা থুংলে	Chatlâidamdâ jhahâj atôppâ amâ thunglê.
It is time to get up	হৌগৎপা মত্তম ওঈরে	Haugatpâ mattam oîrê.
Until this time why are you not done	হৌজিক ফাওবা করিগী থবক লোঈদরিবগে	Haujik fâobâ karigî thabak lôidaribagê.
He has been to visit me three times	ঐবু উনগে হাইদুনা মানা অহুমলক লাকই	Aibû unagê hâidunâ mânâ ahumlâk lâki.
I am tired of correcting this writing	লাঈরিক সেমনবা অসিনা ওইরে	Lâirik semnabâ asinâ ôirê.
He is going to Calcutta	মা কলকতাদা চৎকেতৌরে	Mâ kalkatâdâ chatketaurê.
He has goods to sell	মাগী য়োন্নবা পোৎ লৈ	Mâgî yônnabâ pôt lei.
Give this to the gentleman	পোৎ অসি সাহেবতা পিয়ু	Pôt asi sâhebtâ piyu.
Sew these together	অনিমক অসি তুসিল্লু	Animak asi tusillu.
He is a tolerable workman	খুৎনাঈবা অসি মহৈ	Khutnâibâ asi mahei.
Will you do it to-day or to-morrow	মাসি ঙসি তৌগেরা হয়েং তৌগেরা	Mâsi ngasi taugerâ hayeng taugerâ.
You may come too	নঙবুসুং লাকহন্নিঙই	Nangbûsung lâkhanningi.
You are too talkative	নঙ য়ামনা ৱা ঙাঙগল্লি	Nang yâmnâ wa gnânggalli.
This plank is too long	উপাক অসি সাংমল্লি	Upâk asi sângmalli.

English.	*Manipuri in Vernacular.*	*Manipuri in English Character.*
He took him up for a thief	মাবূ হুরানবনি হাইদুনা ফারে	Mâbû hurânbani hâidunâ fârê.
There is a bird on the top of that tree	উ অসিগী উতোন্দা উচেক লৈ	U asigî utôndâ uchek lei.
Do not touch anything	পোৎ অমত্তসুং সোক্কনু	Pôt amattasung sôkkanu.
He went towards the ghat	হিদেল্লোমদা চৎখ্রে	Hidêllômdâ chatkhrê.
I cannot travel this road	ঐ লম্বি অসি চৎপা ঙমলোই	Ai lambi asi chatpâ ngamlôi.
He speaks truly	মা অচুম্বা হাই	Mâ achumbâ hâi.
Truly, you are a wise man	চুমই নঙ লৌসিং সিংবা মিনি	Chumi nang lausing singbâ mini.
Turn over the leaf	লামাই ওন্থোকউ	Lâmâi onthôku.
Try to play on the flute	বাসি খোংদুনা য়েংউ	Bâsi khôngdunâ yengu.
Turn it over. Turn it round	মাসি ওন্থোকউ। লৈয়ূ	Mâsi onthôku. leiyu.
He shot at the tiger twice, but missed him.	কৈবূ অনিরক কাপই তৌইগুম্বসুং অনিরকমক পান্দে।	Kaibû anirak kâpi tauigumbasung anirakmak pândê.
Give the umbrella	পে পিয়ু	Pê piyu.
The elephant is uncommonly large	সামুনা চাওবা হৌনবদগী হেন্না চাওই	Sâmunâ châobâ haunabadagî hennâ châoi.
It is under the house	মাসি য়ুমগী মখাদা লৈ	Mâsi yumgî makhâdâ lei.
He has gone under water	মা ইসিংদা লুপখ্রে	Mâ isingdâ lupkhrê.
I did not understand	ঐ খঙবা ঙমদ্রে	Âi khangbâ ngamdrê.
Do you understand Bengali ?	নঙ ময়াংলোন খঙব্রা	Nang mayânglôn khangbrâ ?
I understand carpentry	ঐ উসাবগী থবক খঙই	Ai usâbagî thabak khangi.
Unfasten this	মাসি পুনবা থোকউ	Mâsi punbâ thôku.
Wat makes you unhappy ?	নঙ করিগী পুকনিঙ বাবগে	Nang karigî pukning wâbagê ?

These two roads unite near the river	লম্বি অনিমক অসি তুরেনগী মনাক্তা তিল্লি	Lambi animak asi turengî manâktâ tilli.
It floats upon the water	মাসি ইসিংদা তাওই	Mâsi isingdâ tâoi.
You will upset the boat	নঙ হি ওন্থোককনি	Nang hi onthôkkani.
I have no use for this	অসিগী দমক ঐ ইথৌ লৈতে	Asigî damak ai ithau leite.
I have a great variety of goods for sale	য়োন্নবা পোৎ ঐঙোণ্ডা পোৎসক য়ামনালৈ	Yônnabâ pôt aingôndâ pôtsak yâmnâlei.
The ocean is a vast expanse of water.	সমুদ্রদি ইসিং য়ামনা চাওই য়ামনা পাকই	Samudradi ising yâmnâ châoi yâmnâ pâki.
Is not this a very bad house?	মাসি য়ামনা ফত্তবা য়ুমনত্রা	Mâsi yâmnâ phattabâ yûmnatrâ ?
What wages do you receive per month?	থা খুদিঙদা তলপ রূপা কয়া ফংবগে	Thâ khudingdâ talap rûpâ kayâ phangbagê ?
What do you want?	নঙ করি নিঙবগে	Nang kari ningbagê ?
I want nothing	ঐ করিসুং নিঙদে	Ai karisung ningdê.
I want a washerman	ঐ ফিসুবি অমদং পাম্মি	Ai phisubi amadang pâmmi.
He gave me a rupee wanting two annas.	ঐ ঙোন্দা রূপা অমদগী আন্না অনি তানা পিরে	Ai ngôndâ rûpâ amadagî ânnâ ani tânâ pirê.
It is warm	হৌজিক সাওরী	Haujik sâorî.
Wash these handkerchiefs	চিন্দৈ ফি সিং অসি সুদোকউ	Chindei phi sing asi sudôku.
Wash them with water	ইসিংদা সুদোকউ	Isingdâ sudôku.
When washed, spread them out in the sun.	সুদোক তুনা নুংসাদা ফৌদোকউ	Sudôk tunâ nungsâdâ phaudôku.
You must watch the house when I am gone.	ঐনা চৎলগা নঙ য়ুম সঙলম্মু	Ainâ chatlagâ nang yum sanglammu.
Do it any way you like	নঙনা নিঙবা তৌ	Nangnâ ningbâ tau.

English.	*Manipuri in Vernacular.*	*Manipuri in English Character.*
We were going to walk	ঐখোই চৎকে তৌরম্লি	Aikhôi chatkê tauramli.
What does that man wear?	মি আসি করি সেৎপগে	Mi âsi kari setpagê?
He wears a waist-cloth	মা ফৈজোম সেৎলি	Mâ faijôm setli.
What does the woman wear?	নুপি অসি করি ফি সেৎপগে	Nupi asi kari fi setpagê?
Weigh those onions	টিলৌ পুম নমক অসি খল তম্মু	Tilau pum namak asi khal tammu.
If you pay the debt, it will be well	নঙ লমন সিংলবদি ফগনী	Nang laman singlabadi fagani.
Take care, and do this well	সোইফদে চেকসিন্না য়াম্না ফনা থবকতৌ	Sôifadê cheksinnâ yâmnâ fanâ thabak-tau.
Wash them well	অসি খৈবিক সেংনা সুদোকউ	Asi khaibik sengnâ sudôku.
He went in a boat	মা হিদা চৎখ্রে	Mâ hidâ chatkhrê.
We have come from America, the great western island.	আমরিকাদগী নোংজুপ লোমদা লৈবা ইথৎ অচৌবদগী ঐখোই লাকই।	Americadagî nôngjup lômdâ leibâ ithat achaubadagî aikhôi lâki.
Do not let it get wet	মাসি ইসিং চোৎ হনগনু	Mâsi ising chôt hanganu.
What are you doing?	নঙ করি তৌরি	Nang kari tauri?
What do you bring?	নঙ করি পূরকপগে	Nang kari pûrakpagê?
What does this man say?	মি অসি করি হাইবগে	Mi asi kari hâibagê?
What can I do?	ঐ করি তৌবা ঙমগদবগে	Ai kari taubâ ngamgadabagê?
What is the matter?	করি ওইরবগে	Kari oîrabagê?
Of what is paper made?	করি পোৎনা চে সাবগে	Kari pôtnâ che sâbagê?
I am thinking what to say	ঐ করি বা হাইসিবা হাইনা খল্লি	Ai kari wâ hâisibâ hâinâ khalli.
I fear he will die, whatever medicines he may take.	ঐনা নিঙই হিডাক অমবূ চারবসুং অমবূ চারবসুং সিগনী।	Ainâ ningi hidâk amabû chârabasung amabû chârabasung siganî.

English	Manipuri (Bengali script)	Manipuri (romanised)
When will you return ?	নঙ কদৌঙৈ হল্লককদগে	Nang kadaungei hallakkadagê ?
When he comes, tell me	মা লাকলবদি ঐঙোন্দা খঙহল্লু	Mâ lâklabadi aingôndâ khanghallu.
When I call, come quickly	ঐনা কৌরগা থুনা লাকউ	Ainâ kauragâ thûnâ lâku.
From whence do you get those knives ?	সোরি অসি নঙ কৈদগী ফংবগে	Sôri asi nang kaidagî phang bagê ?
Come whenever you please	নঙনা লাক্কে হাইনা নিঙবা অদুদা লাকউ	Nangnâ lâkke hâinâ ningbâ adudâ lâku.
Where are you going ?	নঙ কদাইদা চৎকেগে	Nang kadâidâ chatkegê ?
Where is the house ?	য়ুম কদাইদা লৈবগে ।	Yum kadâida leibagê ?
We reside where we can raise paddy most easily.	মফম অদুদা লৌ উবা য়াম্না চাওবোকই অদুনা ঐখোই লৈবনি ।	Mapham adudâ lan ubâ yâmnâ châobôki adunâ aikhôi leibani.
I was thinking whether he would go	মানা চৎকনী চৎলোই হাইবা ঐ খলহৌরে	Mânâ chatkanî chatlôî hâibâ ai khalhaurê.
Which is the best ?	খাইদগী কদাইনা ফবগে	Khwâidagi kadâinâ phabagê ?
Which do you like ?	কদাই পাম্বগে	Kadâi pâmbagê ?
The law which men should observe	লাইরিকনা হাইবা বায়েনবু মি খাইনা ইনবা থোকই ।	Lâiriknâ hâibâ wâyenbu mi khwâinâ inbâ thôki.
Do not smoke cigars while you are in the house.	য়ুমদা লৈবদা হিডাক থকনু	Yumdâ leibadâ hidâk thakanu.
He came while you were asleep.	নঙনা তুমলিংঙৈদা মা লাকই	Nangnâ tumlingaidâ mâ lâki.
Who is at the door ?	থোঙদা কনা লৈবগে	Thôngdâ kanâ leibagê ?
The boy who has told a lie must be whipped.	মিনম্বা বা হাইবা অঙাং মচাবু য়েবা থোকই	Minambâ wâ hâibâ angâng machâbû yeibâ thôki.
Whoever does evil, must be punished	ফত্তবা তৌবা মিসিংবু দণ্ডি তৌবা থোকই	Phattabâ taubâ misingbû dandi taubâ thôki.

English.	*Manipuri in Vernacular.*	*Manipuri in English Character.*
Give me the whole	ঐঙোন্দা পুম নমক পিয়ু	Aingôndâ pum namak piyu.
The paddy is wholly destroyed	ফৌ পুম নমক মাঙলে	Phau pum namak mânglê.
To whom shall I give it?	মাসি কনাদা পিগদবগে	Mâsi kanâdâ pigadabagê ?
Whose knife is this?	সোরি অসি কনাগীনো	Sôri asi kanâgînô ?
Why do you laugh?	নঙ করিগী নোকপগে	Nang karigî nôkpagê ?
Why do you cry?	নঙ করগী কপ্পগে	Nang karigî kappagê ?
Why did you not bring it?	নঙ করিগী পূরক তবগে	Nang karigî pûrak tabagê ?
Will you go when the tide rises?	জ্বার কারকলগা নঙ চৎকদ্রা	Jwâr kâraklagâ nang chatkadrâ ?
I will not come	ঐ লাক লরোই	Ai lâk larôi.
He will not give his boat	মাগী হি রাইবা পিরোই	Mâgî hi wâibâ pirôi.
The wind blows very hard	নুংসিৎ য়ামনা কন্না সিৎলি	Nungsit yâmnâ kannâ sitli.
Open the windows	মিহুৎথোঙ হাংদোকউ	Mihutthông hângdôku.
Wipe the lamp	মিংসেন থাওমৈ তকথোকউ	Mingsen thâomai takthôku.
When you have wiped, light it	তকথোক লগা থাওমৈ থানগৎলু	Takthôk lagâ thâomai thângatlu.
I wish milk every day	ঐ নুমিৎ খুডিঙ সংগোম পামই	Ai numit khuding sanggôm pâmi.
I do not wish to see him	ঐ মাবু য়েংনিঙদে	Ai mâbû yengningdê.
If he wishes to go, let him go	মানা চৎনিঙ লবদি চৎহল্লু	Mânâ chatning labadi chathallu.
He kills with the sword	মানা থাংনা হাৎলি	Mânâ thângnâ hâtli.
He came with the teacher	মানা ওঝাগা লোইননা লাকই	Mânâ ojhâgâ lôinanâ lâki.
Go with that man	মাগা লোইননা চৎলু	Mâgâ lôinanâ chatlu.
He has gone with the boat	মা হিগা লোইননা চৎখ্রে	Mâ hîgâ lôinanâ chatkhrê.
He cannot go without a spear	মানা তা লৈতরবদি চৎপা ঙমলোই	Mânâ tâ leitarabadi chatpâ ngamlôi.

He speaks without knowing	মানা খঙদনা হাই	Mânâ khangdanâ hâi.
He died without waking	মা মিকপ থোকতনা সিখ্রে	Mâ mikap thôktanâ sikhrê.
He stands without	মা মপান্দা লেপ্তুনা লৈ	Mâ mapândâ leptunâ lei.
Go and cut some wood	চৎলু সিঙ খর য়াল্লু	Chatlu sing khara yâllu.
This word has two meanings	বা অসি অর্থ অনি সুই	Wâ asi artha ani sui.
He works for a living	মানা থবক তৌদুনা থবাই হিংই	Mânâ thabak taudunâ thawâi hingi.
Do not tread on that worm	তিল অসি খোঙনা নেৎকনু	Til asi khôngnâ netkanu.
I am not worthy of so much kindness	ঐনা অসুপ চানবিবা মতিক ওইদে	Ainâ asup chânbibâ matik oìdê.
I would like to have a gun	ঐ নোংমৈ ফংজনিঙই	Ai nôngmai phangjaningi.
I would give thirty rupees for one	অমত্তগী দমক রূপা কুনথ্রা পিবা য়ারে	Amattagî damak rûpâ kunthrâ pibâ yârê.
He would not be comforted	মা থেম্বা য়াদে	Mâ thembâ yâde.
You can write well, can you?	নঙ লাইরিক ফজনা ইবা হৈবা নত্তব্রা	Nang lâirik fajanâ ibâ haibâ nattabrâ?
It is wrong to steal	হুরানবা ফত্তে	Hurânbâ fattê.
You have done it wrong	নঙ ফত্তবা তৌরে	Nang fattabâ taurê.
You have brought the wrong kind of seed.	নঙ জাৎ নত্তবা মরু পূরকই	Nang jât nattabâ maru pûraki.
He visits Calcutta once a year	মা চহি খুডিঙদা কলকত্তা চৎলি	Mâ chahi khudingdâ Calcutta chatli.
He came yesterday	মা ঙরাং লাকলে	Mâ gnarâng lâklê.
He has not arrived yet	মা হৌজিক ফাওবা থুংদরি	Mâ houjik phâobâ thungdari.
More is yet wanting	অমুক খর পামই	Amuk khara pâmi.
He yet lives	মানা হৌজিক ফাওবা হিংলি	Mânâ haujik fâobâ hingli.
Look yonder	আসোমদা য়েংউ	Âsômdâ yengu.
Yonder is the boat	আসোমদা হি লৈ	Âsômdâ hi lei.

English.	*Manipuri in Vernacular.*	*Manipuri in English Character.*
Are you younger than he?	মাঙোন্দগী নঙনা চহি নহা ওঈব্রা	Mângôndagî nangnâ chahi nahâ oîbrâ?
Yes, I am younger	হোই, ঐনা নহা ওঈরি	Hôi, ainâ nahâ oîri.
Is he a relative of yours?	মা নঙগী সাগৈরা	Mâ nanggî sâgairâ?
You have injured yourselves	নঙখোই নহৈ নহৈ মাঙহল্লি	Nangkhôi nahei nahei mânghalli.
Youth is the season for improvement.	মথোক মকারকইঙৈদা লৌসিংসুং চাওখৎলি	Mathôk makârakingaidâ lausingsung châokhatli.

MANIPURI PROVERBS.

English.	*Manipuri in Vernacular.*	*Manipuri in English Character.*
MANIPURI PROVERBS.	মৈতৈগী পাওরৌ।	MEITEIGI PAORAU.
1. A man who wants to wash, gains his end when the bridge breaks. (Application—A man may sometimes get what he wants by an accident.)	ইরুনিঙবগা থোংতেকপগা মান্নবগুম	1. Iruningbagâ thôngtekpagâ mân-nabagum.
2. Wear the ring which suits your business. (Our proverb—"Cut your coat according to your cloth.")	থৌ মপায়েংনা খুদোপ সিবগুম	2. Thau mapâyengnâ khudôp sibagum.
3. A short man tries to reach the moon. (Applies to an over-ambitious man.)	লেপনেম্বনা থা লাম্বগুম	3. Lepnembanâ thâ lânibagum.
4. It is like putting a handle to a light measure. (Applies to any one doing an useless action.)	মেরুক্তা মনা পানবগুম	4. Meruktâ manâ pânbagum. NOTE.—The *meruk* is a measure weighing about 10 chittacks, for which no handle is necessary.
5. It is like showing your fist in the dark. (Applies to a coward.)	অমম্বদা খুদুম উৎপগুম	5. Amambadâ khudum utpagum.
6. You might as well put a small oilseed on the horns of a buffalo. (Applies to any impossible action.)	ইরোই মচিদা থোইদিং থম্বগুম	6. Irôi machidâ thôiding thambagum.

English.	Manipuri in Vernacular.	Manipuri in English Character.
7. You are like the man who gropes for a thing in the dark. (Applies to any one undertaking what he cannot perform.)	অমম্বদা পোৎ মাবগুম	7. Amambadâ pôt mâbagum.
8. You act like children playing with dolls. (Applies to persons who trifle with important business.)	অঙাং মচানা লাঈসান্নবগুম	8. Angâng machânâ lâisânnabagum.
9. Show a looking-glass to a blind man. (Applies to a person who pretends to understand something which he is ignorant of.)	মিৎতাঙবনা মিংসেন য়েংবগুম	9. Mittângbanâ mingsen yengbagum.
10. Give a comb to a Sannyasi (who wears no hair). (Applies to a person giving an inappropriate present.)	লমবোইবদা সমজেৎ পিবগুম	10. Lambôibadâ samjet pibagum.
11. You light the lamps when the meeting is over. (Applies to any one who does not act in time, like our proverb—"Lock the stable door when the horse is out.")	কুমৈ লোইরগা থাওমৈ থানগৎপগুম	11. Kumei lôiragâ thâomei thângatpagum.
12. You keep watch after the thief has carried off your property. (Same in meaning as the previous proverb.)	হুরানবা মত্তুংদা মৈরিংবগুম	12. Hurânbâ mattungdâ meiringbagum.

13. You show fight after receiving a caning. (Same as above in meaning.)	য়েনবা মত্তুংদা পামবোম তিংবগুম	13. Yeinabâ mattungdâ pâmbôm tingbagum.
14. A young elephant does not unto Aderstand the rope. (Applies giving any one a task which he cannot perform.)	সামু মচ্চানা থৌরি খঙদবগুম	14. Sâmu machânâ thauri khangdabagum.
15. Like the poor man's last fowl which has taken to the jungles. (Applies to the loss of anything greatly valued by owner.)	লাইরবনা য়েল্লোইবা ৱাবা ওনবগুম	15. Lâirabanâ yellôibâ wâbâ onbagum.
16. Does a prater merely by talking create wisdom? (Meaning, talking does not make a wise man.)	চিনথিবনা লৌসিং সাবগুম	16. Chinthibanâ lausing sâbagum ?
17. A snake goes straight into its hole. (Our proverb—"Don't beat about the bush.")	লিন্না মখুন চঙলাঈদমদা চুম্বগুম	17. Linnâ makhun changlâîdamdâ chumbagum.
18. Send an eel into another eel's hole. (Our proverb—"Set a thief to catch a thief.")	ঙাপ্রুম মখুন্দা ঙাপ্রুম থাজিনবগুম	18. Ngâprum makhundâ ngâprum thâjinbagum.
19. You might as well put a ring on a cat's tail. (Applies to a person who attempts an impossible action.)	হৌদোঙ মমৈদা খুরেন খুবগুম	19. Haudông mameidâ khuren khûbagum.
20. You are throwing flesh into the tiger's mouth. (Applies to a person who trusts a dishonest person with his property.)	কৈ ময়াদা সদুম হুনজিনবগুম	20. Kei mayâdâ sadum hunjinbagum.

English.	Manipuri in Vernacular.	Manipuri in English Character.
21. The lotus flowers in the middle of the mud. (Applies to any one who from a low origin rises to eminence.)	লৈখোম মরকা থম্বান সাৎপগুম	21. Leikhôm maraktâ thambân sâtpagum.
22. You are like the man who loses his way in an open place. (Applies to a person who throws away a good chance.)	অকোক পদা লম্মাঙ নবগুম	22. Akôk padâ lammâng nabagum.
23. You try to build a wall with soft mud. (Applies to any useless undertaking.)	লৈনাংনা পল থিংবগুম	23. Leinângnâ pal thingbagum.
24. You are like the man who breaks into an ant-hole. (Applies to any one who acts incautiously.)	ককচেং মহুম থুগাইবগুম	24. Kakcheng mahum thugâibagum.
25. You are like a man who attacks a bee-hive. (Same as previous proverb.)	খোঈ মহুমদা চৈনা থিনবগুম	25. Khôi mahumdâ oheinâ thinbagum.
26. You see the dirt in another man's eye, but do not see the dirt in your own eye. (Like the Bible parable of the man who sees the mote in his brother's eye, but fails to see the beam in his own eye.)	মমিৎতা পকপা মিৎসাংদি উদরদুনা মিগী মমিৎতা পকপা মিৎসাং উবগুম।	26. Mamittâ pakpâ mitsângdi udaradunâ migi mamittâ pakpâ mitsâng ubagum.
27. You cannot deprive a tiger of its spots. (Our saying—"Can a leopard change its spots?")	কৈনা ময়েক মাঙব্রা	27. Keinâ mayek mângbrâ.

28. A cat cannot keep quiet while the cooking pot is near. (Application—"Never trust a doubtful character.")	হৌদোঙ তুমিল্লৈবনা চফঙম্বগুম	28. Haudông tumilleibanâ chafangambagum.
29. You cannot hide gold in a rag. (Application—"An able man is sure of promotion.)	সনাবু ফদিনা য়োম্বগুম	29. Snâbû phadinâ yômbagum.
30. He is like the dog which bites without barking. (Applies to a man who speaks ill of you behind your back.)	খোংদনা চিকপা হুইগুম	30. Khôngdanâ chikpâ huigum.

SPECIMENS OF MANIPURI CORRESPONDENCE.

Letter from His Highness the Mahárája of Manipur to the Political Agent.

English.

To His Honour Major Hailes,
Political Agent.

Greeting,
My dear Friend,

I beg to report to Your Honour that I have received and understood the contents of the letter, dated 26th March, in which you asked for 30 coolies to be given by to-morrow evening for the carriage of sepoys' russud to Tummoo. To-morrow I shall not be able to give them. I shall collect and arrange to supply them in 4 or 5 days, and the coolies do not agree to receive as hire Rs. 2-8 each; they say that they must receive the same rate as all have been in the habit of receiving, otherwise they cannot go.

Manipuri in Vernacular.

মহামহিম শ্রীযুক্ত হেলিস মেজর সাহেব
প্রতিনিধি পোলিটিকেল এজেণ্ট
মহিমাবরেষু।

ঐগি চান্নবা মরুপ

শ্রীযুক্ত সাহেবতা খঙহলথি। ২৬ মার্চগি লাইরিক ফংলদুনা ৱারম তারে, তুমুদা সিফাই সিংগি রসদ্ হোন্নবা কুলি ৩০ দং হয়েং নুমিদং ৱাইদা পিউ হাইরকপা অসিদি হয়েংগি নুমিৎ-তদি পিবা ঙমদবা থোকলে। নুমিৎ ৪।৫ নি অসিগি মনুংদা কৌথৎতুনা হোৎনখিগনি। অমসুং বেগারগি মমলদি বেগার ১। ১দা রুপ৷ ২৷৷০ হাইবা অসিদি হাওসিংনা য়াদে মখোইনা হাইবদি খ্ৱাইগি পিবা হৌনবা অদু পিউ অদুনত্তবদি ঙমলোই হাই।

Manipuri in English Character.

Mahâmahima Srijut Hailes Major Sâheb Pratinidhi Political Agent, Mahimâbaresu.

Aigi chânnabâ marup,

Srijut Sâhebtâ khanghalkhi. 26 Mârchgi lâirik phangladunâ wâram târê, tumudâ siphai singgi rasad hônnabâ coolie 30 dang hayeng numidang wâidâ piyu hâirakpâ asidi hâyenggi numittadi pibâ ngamdabâ thôklê. Numit 4, 5 ni asigi manungdâ kankhattunâ hôtnakhigani. Amasung begârgi mamaldi begâr ama amadâ rûpâ $2\frac{1}{2}$ animakhai hâibâ asidi hâosingnâ yâde mâkhôinâ hâibadi khawâigi pibâ haunabâ adu piyu adunattabadi ngamlôi hâi.

On account of my illness I have not been able to go to see Your Honour. I am much grieved because of this.

I send you my best wishes for your welfare.

Your sincere Friend,

(Sd.) SRIJUT CHANDRA KIRTY SING,

Mahárája, K.C.S.I.

Dated 14th Choitra 1807.

ঐনা নাবা মরমনা শ্রীযুক্ত সাহেব খোইবু উনবা ঙমদবা অসিগি দমক য়ামনা ওাই শ্রীযুক্ত সাহেব মঙ্গল ওইরিগণি নিঙই ইতি।

শ্রীযুক্ত সাহেবকি চান্নবা মরুপ

(সহি) শ্রীযুক্ত চন্দ্রকীর্ত্তি সিংহ,

মহারাজা, কে, সি, এস, আই।

মনিপুর।

শক ১৮০৭, মাহে ১৪ চৈত্র।

Ainâ nâbâ maramnâ Srijut Sâheb khôibu unabâ ngnamdabâ asigi damak yâmnâ ôi Srijut sâheb manggal ôiri-gani ningi iti.

Srijut Sahebki channabâ marup,

(Sd.) SRIJUT CHANDRA KIRTI SING,

Mahárája, K.C.S.I.

Manipur,

Shak 1807, Mâhe 14 Choitra.

Letter from a Native Manipuri Officer to the Political Agent.

To His Honour the Political Agent Bara Sahib I send countless salaams.

I beg to send to you, Bara Sahib Political Agent, countless salaams, and beg to report that there is no news of any disturbance. If subsequently I should get any news, I will report it to your Honour Bara Sahib, and I beg you to pardon any omissions on my part.

Dated 12th Magh 1807.

Your obedient servant.

(Sd.) Kongjengba Pohila.

শ্রীলশ্রীযুং কর্ণেল পোলিটিকেল এজেন্ট বর সাসেবকী মফমদা কোটি২ সলাম তৌজহুনা হংগৎচৈ।

শ্রীল শ্রীযুং বর সাহেব পোলিটিকেল এজেন্ট বর সাহেবকী মফমদা কোটি২ সলাম তৌজহুনা হংগৎচৈ ১মুং সাগী লালগী ৱাদি করি থোইদোকপা লৈতে মতুংদা ৱারান ১।১ লৈরবসুং শ্রীযুক্ত বর সাহেবকী মফমদা রিপোৎ তৌজরক্কনি ১মুং অসোই অঙাম পুম নমক ঙাকপিকনি নিঙজৈ, ইতি সোক ১৮০৭ মাহে ১২ মাঘ মাস।

আজ্ঞাধীন শ্রী কোনজেংবা পহিলা,

সর্দার।

Srila Srijut Karnel (Colonel) Political Agent Bara Sâhebkî maphamdâ kôti kôti salaam taujadunâ hangatchai.

Srila Srijut Bara Sâheb Political Agent Bara Sâhebkî maphamdâ kôti kôti salaam taujadunâ hanggatchai amasung sâgi lâlgî wâdi kari thôidôkpâ leite mattungdâ wârân amâ amâ leirabasung Srijut Sâhebkî maphamdâ ripôt taujarakkani amasung asôi angâm pum namak ngâkpikani ningjei. Iti.

Sôk 1807, mâhe 12 magh mâs.

Ahgiadhîn Sri Kônjengbâ Pahilâ

Sardár.

Letter from Kamal Sing to the Babu.

English.	*Manipuri in Vernacular.*	*Manipuri in English Character.*
No. 24.	২৪ নং।	No. 24.
Greeting to my friend Babu.	মমানুগ্রহকারকেষু।	Mamânugrahakârakesu.
Informs as follows :—	শ্রীল শ্রীবাবুদা খঙহলজৈ	Srila Sri Bâbudâ khanghaljei.
The box for His Honour the Sahib which Golab Sing forwarded has arrived. Besides I have bought and kept by me all the dal, grain, &c., which you ordered me to procure. How shall I manage for coolies to carry these things? The coolies which the sahib told me were coming have not arrived. Please inform me how I am to act.	শ্রীগোলাপ সিংহ সেল্লুংবনা চলান তৌরকপা শ্রীযুৎ সাহেবকী পোৎহাপ্পা বাকস অমা অদুসুং থুংলরে হান্নগী হৱাই চেঙৱাইনা চিংবগি জাই অমা পিরকপা অদুগী মানসুং ঙমনা লৈসিন্দুনা থমলে পূনবা বেগার অসি করম তৌগবা শ্রীযুৎ সাহেবকী বেগার লাক্কনী হাইবসুং থুংলদ্রে অসুমতৌ হাইবা অমত্তা খঙহলবিরকউ, ইতি।	Sri Golâp Singha Sellungbanâ chalân taurakpâ Srijut Sâhebkî pôthâppâ bâkas amâ adusung thunglare hânnagî hawâi chengwâinâ chinbagi jâi amâ pirakpâ adugî mânsung ngamnâ leisindunâ thamle pûnabâ begâr asi karam taugabâ srijut sâhebkî begâr lâkkanî hâibasung thungladre asumtau hâibâ amattâ khanghalbiraku.
Dated 30th Sraban 1294.	সন ১২৯৪ বাঙ্গলা মাহে ৩০ শ্রাবণ মাস।	San 1294 Bângalâ mâhe 30 Srâban mâs.
	নিবেদক	Nibedak
(Sd.) Kamal Sing, Muktiar.	শ্রীকমল সিংহ, মুক্তার।	Sri Kamal Sing, Muktar.

Letter from Moreh Thanadar to the Political Agent.

Greeting to His Exalted Excellency MAJOR W. F. TROTTER, *Political Agent.*	মহামহিম মহিমাসাগরবর শ্রীলযুক্ত মেজর ডবলিউ এফ, ট্রটর পুলিটিকেল এজেন্ট সাহেব মহিমাবরেষু।	Mabâmahima mahimâsâgarabar Srila Srijukta Major W. F. Trotter, Political Agent Sahib Mahimâbaresu.
I send countless salaams to the Bara Sahib, and beg to report as stated below. On the 28th Srabun the Tummoo Phoongy came and said that the Kendat Woon had written a letter to him in which he said that he had been informed by the Pagan Woon that the Manipur road was open, and wished the Tummoo Phoongy to inform him whether this was true. If the road was open, it was well; but if it was closed, (the Kendat Woon) directed that all intercourse between the Manipuris and Burmese must cease. On the Phoongy asking whether his people might go to Manipur, I replied that the General Sahib had passed no orders. I told them that as they were not messengers, they might not go; had they been messengers, they might have gone. With regard to their proposal to go to Manipur, I asked them how it was that	শ্রীল শ্রীযুৎ বর সাহেবকী মফমদা হাজারং সল্লাম তৌজদুনা রিপৎ তৌজৈ। ৱারমদি মখাদা ইজরি শ্রাবণ তারিখ ২৮দা তুমু পুঙগ্রিনা হাইরবা ৱা কেন্দাক উন্না লাঈরিক পিরকই, ৱাদি পগানউন্না মনিপুর লম্ফাওরে হাইরৈ অদুনা তুমু কায়োক চুম্বরা ৱা খঙহল্লকউ ফাওরবদি ফরে, ফাওদরবদি নঙখোই ই পাওতাবা চঙনরগনু হাইরে, ঐগিমি মনিপুর চৎকে হাইবদা ননাই ঐখোইনা খুম্বা জেনরেল সাহেবকী হুকুম লৈতে, লাইবার নত্তবনিনা লাইবার ওঈরবদী চৎহলগনী খুম্মি অদুদা মাখোইনদি চৎকদবগী ৱা অসুম তৌরবদা ননাই	Srila Srijut Bara Sâhebkî maphamdâ hâzâr hâzâr salaam taujadunâ ripat taujei. Wâramdi makhâdâ ijari Srâban târik 28dâ tumu punggrinâ hâirabâ wâ kendâk Woonnâ lâirik piraki, wâdi Pagân Woonnâ Manipur lamphâore hâirei adunâ Tummu kâyôk chumbarâ wâ khanghallaku phâorabadi pharê, phâodarabadi nangkhôi i pâotâbâ changnaraganu hâirê, aigimi Manipur chatke hâibadâ nanâi aikhôinâ khumbâ General Sâhebkî hukum leite, lâibâr nattabaninâ lâibâr ôirabadî chathalganî khummi adudâ mâkhôinadi chatkadabagî wâ asum taurabadâ nanâi

English.	*Manipuri in Vernacular.*	*Manipuri in Egnlish Character.*
although the General Sahib had previous to this written a letter to Maung Pagan Woon and the Guayak Sedo about the seizure of the villagers of Laphoi, Salang, and Nongsong, they had not yet sent any reply. I told them that the statement of the Pagan Woon which he gave out as true, was false, as the General Sahib had passed no orders on this matter.	ঐখোইনা হাইবা মমাঙ ঙৈদা জেনরেল সাহেবনা মাও পগান উন্দা ঙাওক সেদো নঙঙোন্দা লফোই, সোলাং, নুঙসোঙ খোমখিবগী লাইরিক পিববু অসুম তৌই হাইবা ৱা খঙহল দবা করিননো নঙগী পগান উন্না মচিন থিদুনা হাইরূবা ৱাবু ৱা ৱৈনা হাইরৈ ৱা পুম নমক অসি জেনরেল সাহেবকী হুকুম লৈতরী হাইখি	eikhôinâ hâibâ mamâng gnaidâ General Sâhebnâ mau Pagân Woondâ ngâôk sedô nangôndâ Laphôi, Sôlâng, Nungsông khômkhibagî lâirik pibabu asum taui hâibâ wâ khanghal dabâ karinanô nanggî pagân Woonnâ machin thidunâ hâirûbâ wâbu wâ wainâ hâirei wâ pum namak asi General Sahebkî hukum leitarî hâikhi
All is well at the thana here, and a sharp look out is kept.	অমসুং থানা অসোই অঙাম লৈতে, হুসিয়ার সন্ত্রি কন্না তৌরি ইতি।	amasung thânâ asôi angâm leite, husiyâr sandri kannâ tauri.
(Sd.) THOKCHAO KANGPOOREL, Moreh Thana.	(সহি) শ্রীথোকচাও কাংপুরেল, মোরে থানা।	(Sahi) Sri THOKCHAO KANGPUREL, Môreh Thânâ.